POISONING ON PARKER ROAD

ONE FAMILY, TWO DEATHS, AND ALL THE SECRETS IN BETWEEN

LINDSEY DAWSON

outLOUDpress

Copyright © 2025 Lindsey Dawson

Lindsey Dawson asserts her moral right to be identified as the author of this work.

All rights reserved. No part of this publication may be reproduced or transmitted in any form or by any means, electronic or mechanical, including photocopying, recording or information storage and retrieval systems, without permission in writing from the copyright holder.

Published by Out Loud Press

Website: www.lindseydawson.com

A catalogue record for this book is available from the National Library of New Zealand.

ISBN 9781067062309 (paperback)
ISBN 9781067062316 (EPUB)

Cover design: Bevan Tonks
Back cover image: Eric Thompson, just six weeks old when his father died of poisoning in Auckland, is pictured aged 27 in US Army uniform. Photo: Nick Frost collection.

CONTENTS

PART I
Shock   1

PART II
Consequences   81

PART III
Ripples   167

Epilogue: Other characters' lives   261

Sources and gratitude   267
Further reading   271
About the Author   273
Also by Lindsey Dawson   275
Other books by the author   277

CONTENTS

PART I
Shock   1

PART II
Consequences   81

PART III
Ripples   167

Epilogue: Other characters' lives   261

Sources and gratitude   267
Further reading   271
About the Author   273
Also by Lindsey Dawson   275
Other books by the author   277

PART I
SHOCK

CHAPTER ONE

One dark night in 1892, farmer John Moorhead was startled awake. Someone was outside, yelling his name. He struggled out from under the blankets and stamped down his narrow stairs, heart racing.

Only dire emergencies could disrupt a man's sleep when he was tucked up in Ōrātia's hills, west of Auckland. Moorhead ripped open the door and saw an agitated man on a shifting horse. It was Alexander Scott, who had been staying in the house of Moorhead's neighbour, William Thompson.

'Go over to Thompson's for God's sake,' called Scott. 'I believe he's about to kick out. I'm off to fetch a doctor.'

'What's wrong with him?'

'He's having spasms. It looks bad. Get the Carters to help!' And with that, Scott urged on his horse and disappeared down muddy Parker Road. It was sometime around midnight on Sunday, 30 October.

Moorhead hauled on some clothes, his mind churning. How could young William Thompson possibly be dying? He was only thirty-two. Formerly fit and healthy, he'd been ailing for several weeks – his neighbours all knew that. But could he really be breathing his last?

Moorhead didn't want to tackle this crisis on his own. He went to rouse the Carters, who lived about a hundred metres away. Carter wasn't home, but his wife, Eliza, got up to see what was wrong. They made a plan. She would go and get James Parker, another nearby resident, while Moorhead hurried five minutes up the road to alert Scott's uncle, John Wilson. This bad business would surely concern him. But Wilson refused to come. He said he had an aching head and wasn't about to go out into the night, even if it was his own nephew who'd called for help.

So it was just a nervous trio – Parker, Carter and Moorhead – who finally gathered outside the small, wood-planked Thompson house. All was silent as they went down through the garden to its door. Maybe a rūrū* made its plaintive double call up in the hills, but there'd have been no other sound except for their footsteps. Inside, the only light came from a candle on the kitchen table. When they called out to William, whose bedroom was just through the wall, there was no answer. They were soon shocked to find he was not ill but lifeless – utterly still on his bed, with grey lips parted, the eyes dull and empty.

'My God, the man is dead,' said Moorhead.

Parker reached out, felt an arm and said, 'Yes, he is – dead and cold. Cold as clay.' They hovered, unsure what to do.

---

* New Zealand owl: rūrū (morepork) or Tasmanian spotted owl.

'We should at least mark what time it is,' suggested Parker. He pulled out his pocket watch. 'Two-fifteen.' The candle cast its dull glow into the room's shadows. They gazed upon William's face, once so lively, now dreadfully vacant.

'It's strange,' said Parker. 'Scott said he was having spasms. Shouldn't the bedding be more disturbed?'

They knew Thompson had been sick and nauseous for about a month. Eliza's husband would later tell the coroner how severe his vomiting was. William told his friend he often felt 'as if a battle was going on in his inside'. He had complained of sore throats and 'loin pains' and even, said Carter, 'fancied some cows had been rolling over him'. Carter put it down to what he called 'an attack of nightmare'. William had once told him his vomiting had been so violent he was scared he would burst a blood vessel.

Thompson's wife, Alice, had been away in Auckland for two months, awaiting the birth of their third baby. So, Alex Scott had moved out of Wilson's house – he'd been living there for about a year – to stay with William as his self-appointed nurse, cooking his meals and sleeping there overnight.

William now lay on his back in the gloom with a blanket lying smoothly over his torso. His legs stretched straight down to the end of the mattress, the feet oddly pointed. Both arms lay bent on the bedclothes across his chest. His head was lolled to the right, the face placid, a smear of what looked like mustard at the corner of his mouth.

They stepped back. Mrs Carter had no doubt helped lay out a body or two in her time. It was a common task for women then. She would have learnt how to do gentle washing, sprinkle fragrant herbs, and brush hair back from lifeless foreheads, but it was not her place to do anything here. Besides, this death was too strange.

They went into the kitchen, closing the door on the corpse. Dirty cups and dishes were scattered about. Someone later said the place looked as if no woman had ever lived there.

The men agreed the police had to be told. Neither of them had a telephone – a luxury that would take another twenty-five years to arrive on Parker Road – so they decided to hitch a horse to a cart and deliver the news themselves. 'We should first take a note of everything in the room,' Parker said. He thought the coroner would want to know the state of things when they'd first seen the body.

They made a list – taking good care about it – and then they left the body alone. There was no point in staying. After all, nothing could disturb William Thompson now.

CHAPTER TWO

Many years later, on the 126th anniversary of William's death, I am standing by his grave in Ōrātia's sweet little country cemetery. It's a drenching wet, chilly October day, and I'm wondering what happened not only to William but to the family he left behind. I'm about to look for evidence of his descendants in countries far from here, but that is all to come. I've brought a bouquet to put at the foot of his imposing gravestone. Me, who has never even once put flowers on the plaque over my own mother's ashes. The idea of marking graves does not much appeal to me, for it's my belief that our spirits fly far and free when we die. Our leftovers, bone or ash, are just remnants of our time on earth.

Still, I lay down my offering beside another bunch of fresh blooms brought by a new friend, Carolyn Melling. We take photos under our sodden umbrellas and then retreat to the shelter of her home. Built in the 1860s, it is a small colonial house clad with kauri planks – William Thompson's old home. He died under this roof.

There's a fire in the grate and fine old china on the table, and we share morning tea with home-made cake in the room where William used to laugh, chat and play his violin. Carolyn has lived there nearly all her life, and she too is interested in the long-ago death that has drawn us together.

IN THE LATE 1880s, the house was named Sunnydale. William and his wife, Sarah Alice – usually just called Alice – both came from prosperous English families, but they'd decided to try their luck in a new land. Like every optimistic emigrant, they'd been keen to build fresh lives with their two small sons, Alaric and Alfgar. But it had all gone wrong.

Within just a few years William was dead and buried, with Alaric alongside him. The little boy was gone at only four. Children's lives were often tragically short in Victorian times.

But there was nothing common about the passing of William Thompson. He died in his prime in a way so suspicious that it led to a murder trial. There were pages of newspaper coverage in New Zealand and Australia. Shock and grief must have rocked families in far-off England.

Imagine the wagging of tongues. One of the chief questions was, had poor Mr Thompson taken his own life or been murdered?

Carolyn researched and wrote about William's death nearly twenty years before I got involved. I stumbled over the story when I was working on my most recent book, historical novel *Scarlet & Magenta*. As I researched Auckland life in the late 1800s, I stumbled over intriguing old press reports about William's mysterious death. They hung on in my head and when time came for a new project, I decided to take another look. In the Research Centre at Waitākere Central Library I discovered Carolyn's account of the drama, published in 2005. She called it *The Lonely Grave: What happened to the man and the boy buried in this grave in the Ōrātia Cemetery.*

I imagined her as an elderly woman interested in local history, who might well now be deceased. How wrong I was. When I sent an email, she came back in a flash – a lively, cheerful woman who is much younger than me. 'Wow!' she wrote. 'What a surprise! This story has intrigued me for years. I have so much information and I'd love to meet you.'

A few days later I drove to Parker Road and found I already knew it. In the late 1960s I used to chug past its signposted lower end in my tiny white Fiat Bambina as I commuted between those same green hills and my Auckland city job.

Every day I drove down West Coast Road, which was – and still is – a narrow, winding ribbon of asphalt fringed with lush trees and shrubs. Branching off it are smaller streets that angle up into the hills.

The death on Parker Road was a story I'd never heard of. But I now know the identity of the Parker after whom the road is named.

James Parker was an architect turned fruit grower. He would later say in court how reluctant he was to visit the Thompson house when William was sick. He hadn't wanted to go there even when William was well. Parker had long felt, he would tell a judge, that something bad was going to happen there. The thought that it might be murder would not have crossed his mind. Not on that quiet country lane. But very soon, murder would be on everyone's minds.

On my first visit to Carolyn's place, she drove me down Parker Road to the Ōrātia Cemetery to see William's grave. The road is still narrow and winding and would have been little more than a muddy track in the 1890s. Today it's an easy drive. As we zipped down the hill she pointed out properties once owned by other personalities in the drama.

We weren't out for long, however, as a phone call soon had her rushing home. Carolyn's husband, Anthony, was waiting anxiously in the driveway for an ambulance. Her beloved dad, who lived in another house on the family property, had been ill for some time. Now he was suddenly much worse. Not wanting to intrude, I said goodbye and left.

A few weeks later, Carolyn told me her dad had passed away. It was odd, we decided later, that the day on which we met contained echoes of what had happened in 1892 – the ending of a life, a quick dash along Parker Road, and much ensuing sadness.

The William Thompson story grabbed me. I wanted to write about it. I had no links with the family, but in a way that made the project easier. With no personal relationships getting in the way, I could just allow myself to dive in.

Researching the long-term impact of the story also drew me in. Today we hear almost daily about killings, accidents, messed-up relationships, shredded families, many kinds of domestic chaos. For how long do consequences ripple on after such dramas? Could I follow a trail of clues about the aftermath of William's death running right through to the twenty-first century? I went into

Papers Past, the National Library of New Zealand's excellent digital newspaper archives, and started reading.

We know Scott roused the neighbours on the night William died because it was reported in the local daily papers, the *Auckland Star* and the *New Zealand Herald*.

Not recorded, of course, was the gossip that followed. Perhaps unable to sleep after so great a shock, Mrs Carter might have seen a light in the Moorhead house and gone there for some company. It's easy to imagine the ladies stoking the fire in the kitchen stove, and maybe fortifying themselves with a nip of brandy as they discussed Thompson's strange illness and the prolonged absence of his wife.

At twenty-seven, Alice Thompson was pretty and petite. William had his own sweetly foolish nickname for her – Tall.

Six weeks earlier she'd given birth to a son in Newmarket, twenty-two kilometres away, at the home of a nurse called Helen Saul, who offered room and care to pregnant women. Alice had gone there along with her other little boy, Alfgar. She had still not returned home after her 'confinement'.

Alice was not just absent from the house but possibly from her marriage, for it was said the couple had been sleeping in separate bedrooms for some time. Her name appeared in reports about William's strange death, but that's all anyone knew. Never called to give evidence, her voice was not heard and her innocence would very soon be fiercely debated.

The neighbours knew William had made a trip into town to see his newborn infant only once, when the baby, named Eric, was just a few days old.

He'd been hale and hearty then, delighting in his tiny boy. Mrs Saul would later testify that he laughed and seemed to be enjoying himself. His harrowing final illness would soon strike, but he was feeling fine that day.

It must have been a welcome bright spot, as it was less than two years since the Thompsons had lost their precious first son, Alaric. Alice often took flowers to his grave. With her own family in distant England, her little one's awful death must have been almost unendurable.

William's focus turned to his apple trees. People said he was enthusiastic but struggling. However, he seemed proud of his place. 'He took a great interest in his farm, and always delighted in showing visitors over it,' said the *Herald* after his death.

He also had music for solace. He was a member of the local brass band, and about three times a week his neighbour, Carter (also named William), came over so they could play violin together. Carter didn't visit so often when Mrs Thompson was there. Maybe he felt he shouldn't disturb family life or perhaps Alice wasn't welcoming.

Now, in late 1892, she was about to face a new calamity. She'd already lost a son, and now her husband was dead too – though she didn't know it yet.

The Moorhead and Carter wives would have pondered on all of this. They might also have talked about the new baby. With his daddy now dead and his mother unlikely to run the orchard alone, who knew where little Eric would be raised in future. The ladies might have muttered about how Alex Scott had often said he intended to bring a doctor out to see the sick man, but never had.

There was poison to discuss, too. John Wilson had revealed that Scott had bought various poisons around town under Wilson's name as well as his own. Why would he do that? And how could Wilson abide his nephew using his own identity?

The story was that Scott had bought arsenic-based poison called Rough on Rats* to kill stray feral cats. Everyone knew to be careful with that stuff. People had been killed, sometimes intentionally – jokesters sometimes called it 'inheritance powder'.

But what had really happened? Scott had told people William was so miserable that he'd talked of taking leave of his life. Might he have poisoned himself? He was making hardly any money from his orchard. He had unpaid bills – and wife troubles. Oh yes, they all knew *that* on Parker Road.

Soon the sky would lighten to the east. This new day would mark the end of William Thompson's life and the beginning of a story that would soon fill columns of newsprint.

It would be called 'The Waikomiti Mystery'.

---

* Rough on Rats was an arsenic-based poison, with coal added for colouring, used to kill vermin. First developed in New Jersey in 1872, it became a common cause of suicide – and murder – in the late nineteenth century. An unsolved Wellington poisoning of a Miss Letitia Stoney is described at http://nzetc.victoria.ac.nz/tm/scholarly/tei-NHSJ07_02-t1-g1-t8.html

CHAPTER THREE

In the 1890s, Waikomiti was a tiny village serving Ōrātia farmers and householders. It had its own railway station and was also home to a huge burial ground. With the spelling changed, it is now known as Waikumete Cemetery* and is New Zealand's largest graveyard. The rail track running alongside it was laid in 1881 to link central Auckland with its western outposts, and the original wooden railway station building (long since renamed Glen Eden) is still in use.

Settlers had started trying to grow fruit in the area as early as 1853, but the clay soil was poor. When Thompson bought there in 1889, he planted five hundred apple trees that failed to thrive.

At least the land had already been somewhat tamed. That was done four decades earlier when sixteen-hectare lots (forty acres) were granted to new British immigrants. William's modest house

---

* Waikumete Cemetery history, https://teara.govt.nz/en/photograph/16137/waikumete-cemetery

on Parker Road was already close to thirty years old when he first laid eyes on it.

The Thompson's house, 'Sunnydale', shown in 1910, about 20 years after William's death. It was 'modest', said a reporter, but its contents indicated owners 'of culture and refinemement'. Photo: Carolyn Melling collection

He was hopeful but clueless. Neighbour James Parker would later say he was 'a square peg in a round hole' and 'would have made a much better living had he had a better knowledge of farming'. William had some income, Parker thought, 'but not enough to live on'.

Growing good apples was hard then. Fruit could be ruined by black spot or drilled through by codling moths that left rotten trails through crisp flesh. Caterpillars gnawed leaves, buds and fruit, webbing the leaves with sticky silk, and William probably spent hours inspecting his orchard for signs of tiny woolly aphids. They gathered in dense, creeping colonies to chew and suck on bark, leading to the growth of galls that made trees sicken and die.

Had Alice heard of galls before she became an orchardist's wife? If she had asked her husband about them, he might have told her they were tumours. It is not just humans who can fall prey to such diseases.

When William and Alice married in the English Midlands in the winter of 1885, they couldn't have guessed that half a decade later they'd be living on the world's far side on a property fringed by 'bush'. This was the local word for the dense tangle of rainforest that still covered fifty per cent of New Zealand when European settlers arrived in the nineteenth century.

The bush on the slopes above the Thompson orchard would have seemed very wild and foreign – slushy underfoot in winter, full of huge trees and tangled with vines and ferns.

It was also a long way from the centre of Auckland. Twenty-two kilometres is nothing to us now, but then it was far from town. Tracks were lumpy in summer and often nightmarish in winter after heavy rain, when even bullock carts got bogged down in sticky mud.

The railway line was a small blessing. The Waikomiti station was a little over six kilometres from the Thompsons' orchard, but there were only three trains a day. They were a motley mix of goods wagons and small, spartan, unheated passenger carriages. Seats were set sideways along the walls, so people slid back and forth with every jerk of the train. First and second class were much the same, the only extra comforts in First being coir floor mats and horsehair cushions on the otherwise bare wooden seating. The carriages were lit with 'colza' lamps, fuelled by rapeseed oil.

Summers usually had long dry spells, but winter tended to deliver lots of rain. Boots and skirt hems were never clean for long. Still, new arrivals might have noticed the freshness of the air.

The Thompsons both came from ancient British towns where the air was laden with distinctive smells. Alice grew up in Walsall, Staffordshire – a town that churned out leather equipment for horses. Every enterprise needed horsepower then for transport and haulage. Rail services were expanding fast, but in the 1880s, ten thousand Walsall workers were still producing all the horse tack anyone could want.

Alice's father, James Hampson, ran a global business as a saddler and lorimer. His workers made harnesses, bridles, bits, spurs and stirrups in a large four-storey factory. He had customers in Europe, the United States, Canada, Australia and New Zealand. Pungent smells from tanneries, forges and workshops must have permeated everything.

William grew up thirty-four kilometres away in Burton-on-Trent, famous then (and now) for beer making. When writer Alfred Barnard went there in 1887, he noted how 'a smell of beer and the odour of hops pervaded the air'.

Beer made William's father, Francis, prosperous too. Burton-on-Trent was famous for pale ale, and the whole world wanted it. The Thompson brewery would merge with another in 1898. Now known as Marston's, it is one of the largest producers of beer in the UK today.

William had three brothers and might have done well in the family firm. But he was the third son and his elder brothers were already working in the business. William was destined for the law. Charles, his younger brother, would become a doctor.

Maybe Francis Thompson was one of those hard-driving fathers with big ambitions for his younger sons. William was sent to Oxford University, but studying would not have been in Alice's life plan. A few women attended lectures there but were not allowed to graduate, no matter how brilliant they were. That ban wouldn't change until 1920. Alice probably had basic schooling and hoped to marry well. Once girls like her became wives, they were expected to be content with motherhood and domestic life.

Sweet-faced young Alice, later to be scorned by a judge as 'a woman lost to every sense of decency'. Photo: Nick Frost collection

Perhaps both of them struggled in those roles. William didn't want to be a solicitor. It was a pity, Charles said after William's death, that his brother had been 'put into the law' as it was farming life that made his heart sing. But Victorian fathers could be forceful and William obeyed.

He was still a student when he married. The wedding took place in December 1885, in eight-hundred-year-old St Matthew's in

Walsall, with family and guests no doubt warmly dressed to fend off the church's winter chill.

The reception was likely a rather grand affair, given both families' prosperity – and no doubt there was Thompson ale on hand for toasting the newlyweds.

William was a catch, with his solid background. Alice was then twenty-one. A studio photo shows her gazing dark-eyed into the camera. Her hair is all frothy curls over her forehead, pulled neatly back into a bun. She has wide-set eyes, a sweet mouth and a small chin. Her shoulders are modestly wrapped with a lace fichu, which was a light scarf pinned over women's bodices to hide any unseemly flesh.

How fortunate she'd have felt on her wedding day. In wooing and wedding her, well-heeled William promised lifelong devotion. He earned his BA the following year at age twenty-five.* Just over seven years later he would be in his grave, and a judge would be thundering to a packed courtroom on the far side of the world that the pretty girl William had married was now 'a woman lost to every sense of decency'.

---

* William's BA degree is listed in an online archive titled *Alumni Oronienses: The Members of the University of Oxford, Their Parentage, Birthplace and Year of Birth*.

CHAPTER FOUR

The newlyweds stayed on in Oxford as William tackled the legal grind. But everything changed when his older brother John and sister Mary went on a grand global tour that included New Zealand and Australia. Leisure travel was only for the rich then, and John and Mary, both unmarried, were lucky to have enough time and money to enjoy it.

John's travel diary still exists in family archives, and it shows he was a man of means. His luggage included three overcoats, five suits (one dress, one serge, two tweed and one black), plus two flannel suits, white linen suits, three pairs of pyjamas, six hats and eight pairs of boots, along with two deck chairs, one gun case, an umbrella, a hat box, a hammock and boxing gloves.

No record survives of Mary's travel notes, but John's reveal his hunting and shooting habits. People he met are barely mentioned, even though they included an uncle on their mother's side – John Hall, a chemist with a thriving pharmacy business in Thames, a gold-mining town east of Auckland. John Thompson admired lively racehorses, went shooting for duck and pheasant and enjoyed some dancing. He was impressed by the good health and demeanour of the Māori but was unimpressed by the colony's roads. 'Horrid', he scribbled in his diary. When his ship tied up in Auckland's harbour on the night of 26 April 1886, he noted it was a town 'badly lighted but quiet'.

In June that year, while William was graduating from Oxford, John was losing his gold watch. It was filched from his room at the Star Hotel in Albert Street when a long-armed thief reached through venetian blinds behind an open window and plucked it from his bedside table.

John also wrote in his dairy that month of being shaken by the 'fearful eruption of Mt Tarawera', which was clearly heard in Auckland two hundred kilometres away. He wrote that it sounded like 'discharging artillery with heavy guns'.

He couldn't resist riding off down country to see the damage. Mary went some of the way too, travelling by coach with lady friends. But the volcano didn't put John off. After a two-month stay in New Zealand, he set sail for home full of praise for the fresh, green land down under.

Later that year, William and Alice were invited to a celebration party back at Ivy Lodge, the Thompson family's big home at Burton-on-Trent. It was a welcome-home affair to mark John and Mary's return. John raved to the guests about New Zealand's huge potential. Now there was a land where a young man could make something of himself!

His stories must have lit a fire in William's heart. The very next year, 1887, he sailed away with Alice and their first-born son, Alaric, to make a fresh start in Britain's most distant colony, twelve thousand miles from home. Who knows how Alice felt about it, with no idea of when or even if she would see her family again.

Alice and her second son, Alfgar, in about 1890. He would be only three when his father died. Photo: Nick Frost collection

They were at least cushioned financially. William took with him between £1000 and £2000. That was serious cash then. A skilled English tradesman had to work for sixteen years to earn £2000.* He also had an annual income from home of about £100 – nearly a year's pay for a tradesman then – derived from another £2000 he'd left invested in the family brewery.

A six-room house could then be bought in Auckland for about £240–£250. The population was about thirty thousand. There

---

* Calculation of worth of £2000 sterling in the 1880s comes from https://www.nationalarchives.gov.uk/currency-converter

were railway services, newspapers, horse-drawn trams, a university, a racecourse, skating rinks – and plenty of lively social life. Hardly fifty years old, Auckland had pioneer spirit, was full of ambition, eager to do well and bursting with big egos.

Maybe William had one, too, or was at least keen to be his own man. The Thompsons lived first in Auckland's Ponsonby and then in Ellerslie. Their second son, Alfgar, was born there in February 1889. The move was not a success, though, as William apparently lost money on property.

He then decided on the only life he'd ever really wanted – setting up his own rural paradise – and persuaded Alice to pack up again, head west and get into apple growing. He found what he wanted on Parker Road and the property's title became his in July 1889.

For a while, perhaps, they were happy. But then their world crumbled. Alaric fell ill. A surviving studio photograph taken at John Hanna's Queen Street studio shows him looking sweet and healthy in a sailor suit – a square-faced boy with pale eyes and short blond hair swept to one side of his broad forehead. Though he's little more than a toddler, his chin is already showing the beginning of a cleft. His younger brother, Alfgar, had one too, which would deepen as he grew to manhood.

He'd have been thought of as 'bonny' – well rounded and solid – but not long after that portrait session he got sick. He'd have had nausea, pain, fever and lack of appetite.

Poor little Alaric. I struggled to find out how he died, because his name was wrongly transcribed in library microfiche files. But once I sorted that little problem out, his missing death certificate arrived in my mailbox. It was kidney cancer. His illness lasted between two and four months.

First-born son Alaric, smartly sailor-suited for the camera, not long before he would fall mortally ill. Photo: Nick Frost collection

The most common form of renal cancer in children aged three or four is called Wilms tumour. These days it has a ninety per cent cure rate, but there would have been no good outlook for any kind of kidney cancer in the nineteenth century. Alaric was doomed.

In a place as small as Auckland there were few medical experts to consult. 'Why did we ever come here?' Alice might have moaned, but arguing would have been pointless. Here they were, far from Britain's best medical brains.

The family's doctor, surgeon Edward McKellar,* assisted by Dr

---

* Dr Edward McKellar's obituary in *New Zealand Medical Journal* archives says

Ernest Roberton*, operated, but it was no use. In January 1891, Alaric died. His parents buried his small body in the Ōrātia Cemetery, down the hill from their home.

What heartache they suffered. The Thompsons back in England, mourning far away, sent £50 out to New Zealand to cover the medical bills. Now, less than two years later, Alaric's daddy was dead as well.

They've been lying together ever since in the grave where I laid my flowers. Their names are both on the one tall headstone. Oddly, Alaric's name is wrong, carved into stone as Aldric. And someone messed up the date. It says the little boy died in 1892, a year after his actual passing. Another mystery.

---

he was a master of surgery who studied in Edinburgh, Glasgow, Paris and Germany. He investigated plague conditions in India for three years, but after being afflicted with severe malaria he sought a kinder climate in New Zealand. He arrived in the 1880s and became popularly regarded as dean of the medical profession in Auckland.

* Dr Ernest Roberton studied medicine at Edinburgh and Vienna universities. He held a number of prominent posts, such as honorary physician to Auckland Hospital for thirty years, president of the New Zealand branch of the World Medical Association, co-founder of Diocesan School for Girls and a member of the Auckland Grammar School Board of Governors. During World War I, when in his fifties, he served overseas in the NZ Medical Corps. (Abridged from his obituary, *NZ Herald*, obituary scrapbooks, Auckland Central Library.)

CHAPTER FIVE

William Thompson's death would eventually lead to a murder trial. The Papers Past archives* got me deep-diving into how the story unfolded, and there were pages packed with court testimony. Smudged printer's ink sometimes made it hard to read, but the two local daily papers both had reporters scribbling away every day in court. If I struggled to decipher something in one paper, I could switch to the other to see if I could find a clearer line of type.

How diligent those reporters were, pushing racing pencils across their notebooks. I was drawn to read the *Star*'s accounts because seventy years after its first reports on William's death appeared, the *Star* was where I found my first job in journalism in the 1960s.

As a newbie 'cub reporter' of seventeen, I would sometimes stand on Fort Street at the rear of the building, thrilling to the thun-

---

* Papers Past is free and open to all at https://paperspast.natlib.govt.nz/newspapers

derous racket of the rolling presses as the day's news was printed out, sometimes with my very own words inside. The stink of ink wafted from the loading bays. Bundles of bound papers were thrown to men on the trays of waiting trucks and stacked high. Off went the news for delivery to the suburbs. People had time to read an evening paper then.

Even further back, in the early 1890s, newspapers were devoured for all the juicy stories of the death up Parker Road.

On the night Thompson died, Alexander Scott sped off on a bay mare owned by Martin's Stables in Manukau Road. He'd hired it the day before. Just like today's hire cars, rental horses had to be returned. This one was young and strong, and Scott pushed it hard to fetch Dr Ernest Roberton. The doctor's home-cum-surgery, Cotele House,* was at the top of Symonds Street. It's lined with glass and steel office buildings now but was then a classy residential avenue with wide harbour views.

Cotele served as a small hospital too. I found names of those who entered and left life under its roof listed in the daily papers. It was Roberton's own birthplace. On that night his head wasn't on the pillow for long.

Scott stepped onto the veranda at about 2am and called out, 'Is that you, Doctor?'

Roberton, a single man of about thirty, possibly sighed, resigned to

---

* Cotele House history, https://timespanner.blogspot.com/search?q=Dr+Ernest+Roberton

the fact that it was every GP's lot to be woken in the dead of night. He rolled out of bed and went to his window.

Scott said he needed the doctor urgently because he thought Thompson had done for himself.

'What makes you think that?'

'He's taken poison or something. I found a small bottle by him.'

Roberton was not Thompson's own doctor but he did know the family, for he'd assisted in the futile surgery to try to save little Alaric. He asked Scott if he knew what sort of poison it was. Strychnine, suggested Scott – he'd seen dogs poisoned that way and the symptoms looked similar.

In later trial evidence, Roberton said Scott told him William was not having strong convulsions, but spasms, and was unconscious. And why did Thompson want to kill himself? Scott said Thompson had that very evening threatened to take his life, but Scott had heard it so often he'd taken no notice.

Roberton had doubts about the strychnine story. If Thompson had swallowed it he'd be dead before they got there, he told Scott. But still, he agreed to go.

Scott asked the doctor to telephone Martin's Stables to order a buggy and two fresh steeds. Auckland had a small telephone exchange by then. Numbers had only triple digits. Roberton picked up the earpiece, twirled the handle on the phone's sturdy wooden box and asked to be put through to Martin's at 472.

Meanwhile, Scott pushed on to the stables and slid off the exhausted horse. He needed a buggy, he told the groom. 'A man has poisoned himself. I'm fetching medical help.'

The firm was used to handling urgent calls. James Martin was the city's leading cab owner, with more than a hundred horses and about fifty vehicles for hire. Scott said to send the bill to the Thompsons, climbed into the buggy, slapped the reins and drove back to Dr Roberton's to pick him up.

ON THE WAY out west in the dark they saw a horse and cart going the other way. Scott suggested to Roberton that maybe it was his neighbours taking Thompson to a doctor. Roberton thought not. 'Surely they'd not be so mad as to do that, knowing I'd been sent for.'

The cart *was* carrying Moorhead and Parker, but they were heading to Avondale to find a telephone to call the police. They had with them their list of items found on the scene.

One little bottle was labelled 'compressed chloride of potassium' supplied by a Dunedin chemist, and others contained small amounts of liquid ammonia and eucalyptus from Auckland pharmacies. They'd also noted a spoon, a tumbler, a wine glass, a dish of jam, some mustard and sugar.

All of these things seemed harmless. And yet, after all the talk of poison on Parker Road, they hadn't wanted to miss anything.

The buggy carrying the doctor kept heading up into the hills. As they lurched along, Scott explained again how Thompson had complained of sadness and wanted to do away with himself. And of how the absent Alice Thompson had said there was poison in the house.

He explained he'd been woken that night by an odd noise – a kind of 'rattling through heavy breathing' – from Thompson's bedroom and had gone in to feel his pulse. He was sure his friend was alive then, he said.

'Are you sure it wasn't the beating in your own fingers that you felt?' asked Roberton.

'I know better than that,' protested Scott. It would later emerge he sometimes told people he'd done some medical study at Melbourne University, but no one knew how true that was.

CHAPTER SIX

It was still before dawn when they finished the climb up to the dark and silent Thompson house. Scott led the way inside.

Dr Roberton's fob watch said it was 4am. The neighbours had snuffed out the candle. Scott re-lit it. He stepped into Thompson's room and, Roberton told the subsequent inquest, 'threw up his arms and made some smothered exclamation'.

The doctor took the candle and saw at once that the patient was dead – and may have died some hours before Scott cantered into town. 'There was a very well-marked rigidity about the body,' Roberton later reported. William's hands were cold but his abdomen still slightly warm.

His head full of the suicide story, the doctor looked around for any evidence to back it up. On a bedside chair he found the small bottles the neighbours had already noted. He then picked up the oval jam dish they'd also seen. Beneath it was something that gleamed in the candle's greasy light – a crystal phial with a silver cap, about as long as his thumb. It was the kind of trinket in which a lady might keep perfume. Inside it were a few white crystals. 'What's this?' he asked Scott.

'That's the poison,' Scott said, and although he'd already told Roberton he'd seen a small bottle next to Thompson's bed, he momentarily looked unsure. 'You've not seen it before?' Roberton asked. Scott shook his head.

It's hard to fathom the doctor tasting a possibly toxic crystal, but he tentatively put one to his tongue, found it 'very bitter' and dropped the phial into his waistcoat pocket, intending to test the contents properly later. There was little else of interest – some jam in a spoon with 'no trace of crystals', a few dry and dusty glasses – and a table with a bowl and a soup dish.

Then, once again, William's body was left alone. The two men set off again back into town. Though they'd had almost no sleep, there was much to do. Roberton wanted to call the police to recommend he do an autopsy. And Alice had to be told her husband was dead. Scott volunteered, but Roberton said no. He insisted her own physician, Dr McKellar, should deliver that news.

Scott did as he was told. He dropped off Roberton, picked up McKellar and took him to the Saul house. It was Monday, 31 October. By now the sun was up. McKellar spoke to Helen Saul and *she* told Alice. Nothing is known about how she took it – whether she collapsed, cried or was stoic.

Now, after three months of absence, she finally had to go home. Getting ready would not have taken long as she had earlier told Saul that she planned to leave on Sunday the 30th. But Scott had visited on Saturday the 29th and somehow persuaded her not to.

This meant she was still absent on the night William died. How very odd that was. And even more odd that in all the later investigations, it seems no one thought to ask Scott what he'd said to make her stay away.

There would have been more messing about with transport arrangements. With McKellar's job done, Scott's next task was to take Alice, Helen Saul and the boys out to Parker Road. The morning trip back out to Sunnydale required a bigger vehicle than the one Scott had used overnight. He'd have made another choice from Martin's range. There were landaus, hansoms, hearses, black mourning coaches, beribboned wedding carriages, and wagonettes big enough to take a rowdy group out for picnic parties with their hampers, blankets and the family dog.

But this was no picnic. By the time Scott delivered the widow's party to Sunnydale after a sleepless night, he must have been very tired.

By that time the law had turned up. Constable William Kelly had arrived from Auckland, keen to talk to the widow and to Scott – the man who, in Alice's absence, had stepped into the kind of nursing role that wives usually filled. An undertaker would have been there, too, waiting for Mrs Thompson to view her late husband's body before it was carried away.

The policeman had already gone to the home of Scott's uncle, John Wilson, and smelt the whiff of scandal that hung about Alice. A co-operative Wilson took Kelly into Scott's room, where he knew there was a locked box. They forced it open. Inside they found some small bottles that Kelly commandeered, plus a nearly full box of Rough on Rats poison.

Kelly must have taken in the gossip he heard from Parker Road neighbours about Scott and Alice being unusually 'familiar'.

An *Auckland Star* reporter was also there, writing later that Thompson's widow was in the house, 'and playing merrily about was a fine little fellow five or six years of age, a son of the deceased, happily unconscious of the sad scene that was being enacted in his home'.

Alfgar was actually not yet four, but old enough to remember the house. Where was his daddy? Had he been told his father wouldn't be there? Who were all these strangers? His mother stepped inside and turned right to enter the room where William lay.

Kelly would have watched her closely, noting if she seemed genuinely grief-stricken or was quiet and steely. Did she produce too many tears or too few?

This was the start of a tense and extraordinary two days, during which Alice was humiliated and Scott was hugely compromised.

Alice and Scott, plus Helen Saul, Alfgar and baby Eric, stayed at Sunnydale that night, with Alice thankful for Saul's support. Scott would later say she was by now much more of a 'great friend' than a nurse. The compact house had two levels. Its ground floor had a narrow hall and a staircase up to the attic. The *Star* reported it wasn't grand but the interior showed its owners were 'persons of culture and refinement'. There were oil paintings, a harp, a cello and 'a marble clock stood on the chimney piece in front of a handsome mantel'.

The Thompsons' old fireplace as it looks today – the spot where a neighbour was once scandalised by Alice's flirtatious behaviour. Photo: Joey Tonks

Given Thompson's strange and lonely death it must have *felt* horrible. And who would have wanted to eat anything from that kitchen? There was probably scant food anyway, and no nearby shops to run to. The nearest, several miles away, was just a front-room setup in the house of a trader who used to deliver basic supplies around the district. Maybe neighbours brought over something to eat, or at least offered sympathy and a restorative cup of tea. Country folks usually look after each other and there was the new baby to admire. And little Alfgar must have been tired and hungry after the long trip out from town. These people had comforted Alice and William through Alaric's ghastly illness – and had probably stood with them when his small coffin went into the ground.

But things were different now. Alice had been gone a long time. The other wives might have whispered amongst themselves about her many weeks away. And now William had died and she was here too late, poor woman. With luck, they were kind to her rather than cold.

Alice shared her old ground-floor bedroom with Helen and the children that night, while Scott dossed down on a couch in the dining room, where, more than a century later, I enjoyed coffee and cake with Carolyn. Back in 1892, Alice and the others would have needed to get some rest – the next day would bring more shocks.

William Thompson, whose 1892 death was called 'The Waikomiti Mystery'. No photos were printed in papers then. Only this sketch survives, provenance unknown.

CHAPTER SEVEN

When Constable Kelly returned to Auckland with the items from Scott's box, he told his boss, Inspector Thomas Broham, what he'd seen and heard. Broham left the city early the next day, 1 November, with two of his men. They arrived at the house at about 7.30am.

Another detective, Martin Grace, was also busy that morning, visiting Auckland pharmacists. He wasted no time in asking two of them to join him on the midday train to Waikomiti. Grace was eager to get to Sunnydale. Inquests happened swiftly then, and this one was set to take place there that very afternoon.

Early Auckland had no courtrooms set aside for inquests. Instead, they were held close to the death scene at the nearest place where people could gather out of the weather – often the local pub. Or, as in this case, in the house where its owner had died only the day before. Police evidence was presented and witnesses (if any) told their stories. Unless a crime was suspected, the coroner made a quick pronouncement on how the deceased had passed away and the whole business was soon over.

Alice and tiny Eric had to have been up early. When a baby is only six weeks old, nobody gets much sleep – apart from which, imagine the turmoil in Alice's mind.

BACK IN TOWN, Roberton was about to carry out the post-mortem on William's body. Doctors had to be multi-skilled back then. And with no refrigeration available, an autopsy was best done as soon as possible.

The train track from Auckland was often used to carry coffins containing the newly deceased out to the cemetery close to Waikomiti station. Bodies and mourners often travelled in the same train on their way to funerals – the living in one carriage, the dead in another that was marked with a white cross.

In this case the opposite may have happened. Newspaper reports do not say where the autopsy happened, but it's likely to have been in Auckland's morgue in Freemans Bay that Roberton removed tissue for analysis.

Roberton had already seen a lot of life and death. The son of a wealthy merchant, he'd been sent to universities in Edinburgh and Vienna. A medical degree could not be earned in New Zealand until 1887, so he'd had to get his training elsewhere.

Now well travelled and used to the finer things of life, he steeled himself every time he worked in the morgue because it was a frightful place. Just six months before William's death, he was one of three doctors who had pleaded with the Auckland City Council for a new one to be built.

Someone who'd seen its horrors for himself was a hotel-keeper, Andus Raynes. He had attended an 1890 post-mortem and penned an outraged letter to the editor of the *Auckland Star*.* 'The dreadful nature of the business was rendered doubly sickening by our surroundings,' he wrote. 'One filthy rag, the remains of a towel, was all we had to dry our hands with after washing them in the one basin available for all the purposes of the place. Indeed, we had to use a cloth that had been encircling the corpse.'

Twenty years later, the *NZ Truth* newspaper would *still* be shouting about the morgue's 'dreadful disrespect of the dead'. They called it the city's 'Smellful Scandal'.

But now, working as fast as possible, Roberton did his best. He may have opened Thompson's body with the Y-shaped cut often seen today in crime-show mortuary scenes. It was invented after mourners complained they did not like to see scalpel cuts or stitches when viewing deceased loved ones. Instead, two diagonal incisions were made under the shoulders, converging to carry on down the abdomen as a single central line. This ensured that clothing covered any signs of dissection.

On 1 November 1892, Roberton removed William's stomach and portions of the liver, spleen and each kidney, as well as part of the contents of the large intestines. They went into glass bottles that were to be taken to Colonial Analyst James Pond for testing, along with the little glass phial. The doctor had already tested some of

---

* Auckland morgue, Raynes' full letter, https://paperspast.natlib.govt.nz/newspapers/AS18900802.2.32

the crystalline content of the phial himself and found it to be strychnine, but Pond was the official expert.

One day later, William would be buried back at Ōrātia Cemetery on West Coast Road next to his first son, Alaric.

The tall gravestone marking Thompson deaths is so old now that the names are hard to read – but here lie William Thomposn and his small son Alaric, misnamed as Aldric. Photo: Joey Tonks

As Roberton carried out the post-mortem, a new drama was happening on the attic floor of the Thompson house. Two policemen went upstairs with Scott. With the inquest due to start in just a few hours, they were still searching for evidence. Wilson, Scott's uncle, had told them his nephew had taken a black bag from his room. They wanted to know what was in it and suspected Scott may have carried it to Sunnydale. Indeed he had.

'There it is,' said Scott, pointing to a small, glazed bag. It was empty. He'd only used it for a change of clothes.

Detective William Chrystal asked if he could search Scott's pockets and found some letters. 'They're all Mrs Thompson's,' said Scott. 'She gave them to me last night to keep them for her.'

There was more – in the pocket of an extra pair of trousers in the room was a small, round cardboard box. Chrystal removed its lid. Inside was a birth-control device called a 'preventative pessary'*,

---

* Chemist WJ Rendell is credited with inventing the first commercial pessary in 1880. It involved a sea sponge, quinine and cocoa butter. Pioneering birth-control complete with a diagram and instructions for its use. 'That's private!' said Scott. 'I purchased it for a young lady. I must have it back.'

He tried to grab it and they struggled. 'Mrs Saul! Mrs Saul!' Scott shouted. She didn't come, but Alice ran up the stairs and instantly saw the box.

'That's mine,' she pleaded. 'I gave it to Mr Scott to keep for me. You mustn't take it away.' But Chrystal did. Months later, it would be solemnly passed from hand to hand in court so twelve male jurors could see it for themselves while a judge observed, 'The jury may or may not know what these things are.'

Birth-control devices were intimate feminine items, and it was shocking that Alice had asked a man who was not her husband to mind it for her. Many Victorian families were so large (a brood of nine or ten wasn't uncommon) that we assume women had no way of preventing conception. But of course they tried, using douches, sponges and pessaries. These were usually a dome-shaped cup inserted into the vagina as a sperm-collection device. Alice may have had a popular British model called Dr Patterson's Inflated Rim Check Pessary, which had a hollow rim inflated with air. 'It has the advantage of being beautifully soft,' said an advertisement, 'so that when adjusted as directed it is almost impossible to feel its presence.' The pessary came in a box for two shillings and sixpence.

There was still another electrifying moment to come. Detective

---

activist Annie Besant was so impressed that she recommended their use to women wanting to limit their families. By the turn of the century they were being sold worldwide. Even long after his death, later versions were sold under his name in the 1930s with the slogan 'Wife's Friend'. https://teara.govt.nz/en/object/26977/pessaries

Grace also went to Wilson's house to search Scott's room there, and in a trunk he found two women's chemises. Garments like these were worn close to the skin. Loose-fitting and made of fine linen or cotton, they went under corsets to protect clothing from sweat. Why, the policemen wondered, did Scott have women's underwear in his room?

CHAPTER EIGHT

The inquest into William Thompson's death would go on for days at another venue, but it started in Sunnydale's living room on the afternoon of Tuesday, 1 November, with onlookers pressed in amongst the musical instruments and song sheets.

Alice was still in the house, though not in the room, and probably still in shock. She'd seen her husband's dead body only the day before. Women were barred from attending inquests then. Reporters saw her walking around and the *Herald* described her as 'slight and of an attractive appearance, showing every indication of refinement and culture'. The attractiveness of the men was, of course, not mentioned.

Six locals were appointed as the jury. Inquest juries could wield a big stick, despite being only six 'good men and true' instead of the customary twelve. One of the jurors was a Mr Shaw, whose name also lives on today on another local street sign, Shaw Road. The rest were named Evans, Gill, Bendall, Sharp and Soppett. With so few settlers in the district, they all likely knew each other, as well as being acquainted with Thompson and Scott.

A little before three o'clock, even as the policemen were still gathering evidence, Coroner John Bollard got down to business.

THE FIRST WITNESS WAS SCOTT, the last man to see Thompson alive. He'd come to stay with his uncle late in the previous year of 1891. Scott had known William for about ten months, he said, and for most of that time they had been 'very intimate'. That term was used then to describe any close friendship, whether between men or women.

Alice Thompson went into Auckland on 10 August to await the birth of her third baby, which was expected in the following month. Scott was then still living with his uncle. The baby was born on 18 September, and about a week later, Scott heard that William was ill. He went to see him and found him in bed. He'd been having vomiting spells and asked Scott to stay with him. It was 27 September.

And so Scott did. He stayed on for the next five weeks, often doing the cooking and sometimes leaving prepared meals for Thompson to eat on his own, for Scott was often away in Auckland doing errands, making visits and getting medicines. William Carter regularly saw Thompson too. On Scott's away days he would check on his neighbour, who was sometimes unwell but not stuck in bed. He would get up late in the morning and wasn't back between the sheets until ten or eleven at night. He was fit enough to be outside in the rain chopping wood only three days before he died, according to Scott.

Some of Scott's trips to town were to see Dr Roberton so he could describe William's symptoms and ask for medicines. Scott had tried to get William to go in person to be properly diagnosed, he told the coroner, but the answer was always no – the doctor's bill would be too high.

The *Herald* reported that Scott said Thompson had told him he was 'utterly penniless'. Funds that should have arrived from home had not turned up. He had also suffered 'fits of despondency' following his little boy's death. He had spoken often of 'wanting to put an end to himself', asserted Scott.

The day leading up to Thompson's death was an ordinary kind of Sunday. He snoozed in an armchair for a few hours. The only notable moment was when neighbour John Shaw (the same Shaw who was now sitting on the jury) visited at 4pm to see how he was. Told by Scott that William was sleeping, he went away.

Then came the night. Thompson went to bed at about nine after repeating, according to Scott, his complaint about being sick of life. Scott stayed up smoking for an hour and then settled down on the dining room sofa.

At about midnight Scott heard a noise from Thompson's room and found him in spasms, not speaking, unconscious. Scott tried to give him mustard and water as an emetic but did not succeed. He then ran to saddle the horse, woke up Moorhead and went to fetch Dr Roberton.

Scott said that in previous weeks he had sought help for Thompson not only from Roberton but from pharmacies, too. He'd bought something called 'colonial pills' for William's liver from Jefferson's chemist shop and other 'physic' (medicine) from a firm called Graves Aickin. He said he thought William was taking morphia and admitted he himself used morphia and chloral for sleeplessness.

Chloral, an early sedative drug, was a popular fix for insomnia. Thought then to be harmless, it was actually very addictive. Morphia is another name for morphine, derived from the opium plant and widely used in the nineteenth century – and today – as a pain reliever and sedative.

Scott had bought more items from Jefferson about six weeks earlier, including laudanum, a liquid mixture of alcohol and opium. People saw it as a cure for everything from headaches to menstrual pain, but laudanum addiction was rife in Victorian times.

Scott also asked for arsenic-based Rough on Rats to kill some annoying stray cats, and a small bottle of diluted strychnine. Highly toxic, strychnine is derived from seeds of the tropical nux vomica tree. Scott told the coroner that he'd mixed the strychnine into milk and, when it didn't work, he poured what was left into an ash heap and used a shovel to cover it up. Poisons had to be registered in each chemist's poisons book and Scott duly signed for them.

Then Inspector Broham pounced. 'Did you get those drugs in your own name?' he wanted to know.

Scott had an official 'friend' at the inquest – solicitor Frederick Baume who, said the *Star*, 'watched the proceedings on behalf of the family'. It's not clear who 'the family' was – presumably that of the deceased – or who was paying for his time, but Scott felt the need to whisper to him. He no doubt wanted someone – anyone – to give him advice.

The inspector didn't like it. 'I would ask the coroner that the witness reply to my question and that he be permitted to give his answers without interruption.'

Baume objected, saying the questions were hostile. 'The witness is here and asked to answer questions and it is only reasonable that he should refer to a solicitor before answering.'

The old newspaper reports are confusing because the two men's names – Baume and Broham – are so similar. The policeman, Broham, wasn't giving in. 'Has he only come then to tell part of the truth?'

On they squabbled until Scott conceded that at one pharmacy he'd used his uncle's surname, Wilson, but chosen a random first name. He'd not used his own name, Scott explained, 'for the simple reason that I got into a slight trouble some time ago about a cheque, as Inspector Broham well knows, and I took an alias for the time being. The past is past and gone.'

Broham moved on – he had another card to play. 'Do you know Mr Orr, the chemist?' he asked Scott.

'No.'

Then – surprise! – Orr stepped into the room. He'd just arrived on the train that morning. Scott had to back down. Soon he was confessing yes, he had bought belladonna at Orr's pharmacy, plus more laudanum. And six grains of strychnine. And prussic acid – a liquid and poisonous form of cyanide.

'In what name were the drugs bought?' asked Broham.

Not his own, Scott confessed, but he couldn't say what name he'd used. He'd been 'completely confused' ever since the earlier conversation about his use of a dud cheque.

'Did you tell Mr Orr for what you wanted them?' asked Broham.

Scott wasn't sure, but he did remember he wanted strychnine to kill stray cats, and added, 'The laudanum I took myself.'

A few minutes later he'd probably have preferred a slug of brandy. For as soon as the questioning was over and he stepped outside, Inspector Broham arrested him for murder.

Lawyer Baume stalked furiously back into the crowded parlour. 'I think it is just as well to state,' he announced, 'for the benefit of all concerned, that immediately Mr Scott left this room he was arrested. Inspector Broham must have known he intended to have this man arrested, and yet he gets him here to make a long statement on oath!'

The inspector was indignant. 'I must ask you, Mr Coroner, for protection. Mr Baume has no right to attack me in this manner.'

'If the man was to be charged with a crime of this kind,' replied Baume, 'I say it was against all principle of British justice and right to compel him to give his evidence first.'

The inspector declared himself 'perfectly *amazed*' to be attacked, but Baume was still outraged. 'If this man was to be arrested, you ought not to have asked him a single question.'

'Dear me, Mr Baume,' the inspector replied, 'there is no need to get into a white heat.'

The coroner put a stop to the skirmish. 'Mr Baume, it's a matter between you and the police.'

This was bad luck for Scott because the coroner seemed unconcerned with the right to silence. An accused person or defendant could refuse to comment or provide an answer when questioned, either before or during legal proceedings – a right that had been a hallmark of British law for at least two hundred years.*

AFTER THAT ERUPTION, the inquest stuttered on. Wilson was no doubt alarmed his nephew was now under arrest for murder, but he'd hardly have been surprised. His sister (Scott's mother) had visited from Australia at some point and had thought her son was too attentive to Alice – 'hanging to her tail too much', was how she put it. When Wilson had heard Scott was buying poisons, he had even written to his own solicitor to ask if he could discover the truth of these stories, saying he 'was afraid he [Scott] might do himself or others harm.'

Scott had not said he was planning to kill stray cats, but Wilson had seen one 'frothing at the mouth' and thought it must have eaten a poisoned bird.

Settlers saw sparrows as pests then. After being introduced to New Zealand by English immigrants who missed the sweet little birds of 'Home', sparrows, finches and skylarks had multiplied. By the 1880s they were plundering gardens and farms. Householders wanting to get rid of them could simply buy poisoned wheat and scatter it around. Seeing the cat in agony made Wilson afraid for his dog and he kept it tied up.

But it seemed Scott himself made Wilson uncomfortable. His nephew had 'manias and fads', he said. One of them was collecting. 'He might collect saddles and bridles, without any evil intent.

---

* Two hundred years of the right to silence is a modest estimate, as historians have traced it to early canon law and the political conflicts of the sixteenth and seventeenth centuries.

He would pick up anything that took his fancy, such as clothes, buttons and papers, and would store them away.'

He now probably had a fancy to collect poisons. Wilson did not know why. There was also a hint that maybe Scott's mind wasn't well ordered. 'He had brain fever once,' Wilson revealed, 'and also a fall from a horse when at school, and he has never been perfectly right since then.'

CHAPTER NINE

That was that for the inquest's first day. Alice wasn't seen by the men crowding her parlour. Inspector Broham would later say he had asked her about the pretty crystal phial Dr Roberton had found. Was it hers, this little bit of female frippery? Or her husband's? Her answer is unknown, because Broham didn't mention it to the coroner and wrote no report on what she said. Nobody else asked Alice to say anything at all.

She stayed invisible. Anytime she was referred to, the family's lawyer, Baume, stood to object. 'A name of a woman especially ought to be held sacred,' he asserted. Perhaps no one wanted to upset the young new widow. Or perhaps she was left alone because of that newspaper comment about her air of 'culture and refinement'.

The jurymen knew nothing of the upstairs tussle over the scandalous pessary Alice had claimed was hers. They were ignorant of the soft chemises found in Scott's trunk. Inspector Broham knew, because his officers updated him every time he slipped out of the room during Scott's testimony. Those two discoveries, plus some letters also unearthed that day, convinced him that Scott deserved arresting then and there.

It's hard to know what the jurors thought of Alice. Inquests were men-only affairs and she was a stricken and grieving young mother. Maybe the men simply didn't see her as the kind of woman who could be involved in something as vile as poisoning.

By the time Wilson had stopped talking it was 6.15 in the evening. It was a long ride back to Auckland. Alice was driven back to town by Captain John Herrold, a longtime friend of the Thompsons. He'd gone out to Sunnydale as soon as he heard the dreadful news. Sympathetic, and unwilling to leave her in the house for a second night, he arranged for transport back to Helen Saul's home.

Alice possibly never stayed at Sunnydale again. There are no reports of whether she was amongst the small crowd who attended William's funeral the next day in little Ōrātia Cemetery down the hill, with the Rev W Calder officiating.

Perhaps during the journey to the Saul residence she gave way and cried, for she'd heard of William's death one day earlier and Scott was arrested for his murder the next. Alfgar may have been whining and baby Eric howling to be fed. A miserable trip was pretty much guaranteed. Scott, who once used to drive out with Alice, was being escorted to the Auckland police station. On the way he said: 'So help me God, Thompson died by his own hand.'

The next morning he appeared before a magistrate to be formally charged with 'wilful murder'.*

---

* 'Wilful murder' is an outdated expression. New Zealand law now uses the term 'culpable homicide' to refer to either murder or manslaughter. Murder is defined broadly under the law to cover a range of instances when someone kills with the

The *Auckland Star* described him: 'A young man of rather gentlemanly appearance. He's of medium build, five feet nine inches in height. His eyes are bluish-grey and his face is long and rather narrow. Both nose and chin are somewhat prominent, the former being slightly aquiline.' His hair and muttonchop whiskers were black and when arrested he was wearing a grey tweed coat and vest with white trousers.

Newspapers did not yet print photographs, but Scott, the potential villain, appeared in this artist's sketch.

New Zealand Herald *sketch of Alexander Scott. An* Auckland Star *reporter said he was "of rather gentlemanly appearance".*
Illlustration: PapersPast.co.nz

William, the victim, scored only a brief personal precis that said he was 'rather quiet by nature, with light brown hair and a moustache.'

There are no surviving photos of William as an adult. There is,

---

intention to hurt, whereas manslaughter applies when death is caused by an unlawful act but there is no murderous intent.

however, a studio portrait of him, taken when he was a boy back in Burton-on-Trent. His gaze is mutinous. They've given him a toy horse to hold, but you can see his resistance. Neither the photographer nor William's mother (you can feel her presence in the room) has been able to coax a smile from him. He is dressed in a sharply tailored suit and slouches in an ornate chair, dark hair slicked across his forehead. His feet, in fine, shiny leather boots, dangle clear of the floor.

In about twenty years he would leave his privileged life behind to make his own way on the world's far side – a move that would lead to his lonely, harrowing death.

Young William Thompson, apparently not enjoying being told to sit still for the camera. Photo: Nick Frost collection

THE PHOTO CAME to light via Carolyn and her connections with Thompson family members in England. Though William's house has been her home for many years, she has, like me, no family ties to the Thompsons. She always knew a murder had taken place there, but her fascination with the story intensified twenty years ago when others with an interest dropped by.

Carolyn and Anthony were running a plant business on the property. 'One day, two women turned up in a little red car. I thought they were customers.' They turned out to be genealogy enthusiasts. 'They said someone had written to them from England wanting a photo of the old house where a family member had been murdered. They weren't sure if they'd found the right place.'

They had, and showed her the letter, written by a Monica Leat of Ross-on-Wye, Herefordshire. Carolyn began swapping information with Monica, who was William's two-times great niece. Monica was working on the Thompson family tree and had become intrigued by the mysterious New Zealand death. 'The two ladies never did send her the photo of the house,' Carolyn told me, 'but she got me instead.'

They corresponded for years. Monica died in 2010 but her husband, David, later visited New Zealand and saw for himself the place his wife had been so intrigued by.

And now I was wanting to dig even deeper. Carolyn put me in touch with David, and also with another Thompson family member, Nick Frost. He is a great-grandson of John Thompson, whose exciting 1886 holiday in New Zealand spurred his brother William to emigrate.

Nick, who holds many of his family's old records, is the second-generation owner of Frost Antiques in Monmouth, Wales. A specialist in Staffordshire pottery figurines and country furniture, he's a man who cherishes historical objects. He lives on the premises and there have been boxes of old Thompson family history stowed in his attic since 1983. He'd already shared the contents with Monica many years earlier, and soon I was asking if I might see them too.

I wanted to write not only about William's death but also to learn what had happened afterwards to Alice and her boys. The public fuss about the case fizzled out in 1893, when the New Zealand legal proceedings were over. But when William was buried, his widow was only in her twenties and her small sons had their lives left to live. What, I wondered, had become of them?

I expected Nick to say no. What right did I have to rummage in another family's history? But he was curious too, and said his own mother had told him a romanticised version of the murder case. 'She thought William had travelled to New Zealand ahead and Alice travelled later and fell in love with a doctor on board ship – a relationship which continued on land and ended in William's poisoning.' It's not true, of course, but this is how stories handed down through families grow soft around the edges, becoming hazy legends.

Nick kindly offered to unearth the Thompson papers. 'What do you want to see?' he asked.

'Well, anything that relates to William's life and death,' I said, 'and what happened afterwards.' He promised to sort out documents and photos. The Covid pandemic had arrived and sending goods worldwide was a slow and anxious business. After prepaying the freight charge I waited, ticking off the days until a courier would drop it all at my door. Meanwhile, I pushed on with other research.

Scott's background was a mystery, and in a break between Covid lockdowns I flew to his old hometown, Melbourne. Victoria's census records before 1892 were destroyed long ago, but an obliging librarian dug out some birth records preserved on a CD-ROM. And there was Alexander Scott's family! He was the eldest of seven. His parents, Agnes and James, had four more sons in quick succession – William, James, Thomas and Ernest – and, finally, a girl named Florence. Eleven years later, when Scott's mother was forty-four, there was another daughter.

The Scotts lived in Geelong. I later found Mrs Scott's will and probate online. By the time she died at seventy-six in 1909, she'd lost her husband and three sons. The last one was ignored in her will. Only her daughters shared her estate. It was a bare piece of land worth £200 (about $A28,000 today)* and a little furniture.

I was still away when Nick's box of family memories thumped onto my doorstep – a big brown cardboard box. I tore it open as soon as I got home. Smells of old paper, leather and mildew wafted out as I carefully lifted each layer of fragile documents, tissue-wrapped photo albums, letters and memorabilia. All this evidence had come to me in the chilly cargo hold of aircraft not even dreamed of in the nineteenth century.

---

* Australian Pre-Decimal Inflation Calculator, https://www.rba.gov.au/calculator/annualPreDecimal.html

CHAPTER TEN

Alexander Scott and Alice Thompson became entangled about a year before William's death. Alice's sadness must have been profound after losing little Alaric earlier in 1891. But then, up Parker Road rode Alexander Scott, who had come to stay with his uncle.

Scott and both the Thompsons struck up a quick friendship. At evening get-togethers William played merry jigs on his violin, with Scott providing rhythmic backup on 'the bones'. These were shortened flat animal bones held loosely between the fingers to set up a clattering beat. Scott and Alice got along well and then their attraction began to run deeper.

Did people notice? Of course they did.

Washerwoman Bertha Kennerley was only fifteen. She went to the Thompsons' every Monday, when Alice was at home – or fortnightly if only William was there. Bertha appeared at the inquest, probably very nervous. A newspaper sketch shows her hair pinned up beneath a pert little hat. She'd have taken care to look neat and tidy that day, knowing that many men would be looking at her.

Bertha said she knew her employer had been sick in the last three weeks of his life – she'd heard him vomiting. A lawyer wanted to know if she had noticed Scott and Alice Thompson together. Bertha had. She'd seen him take tea to Alice in her bedroom one day when she wasn't well.

Bertha stayed the night there once, before all the trouble began. While Mr Thompson was out at brass-band practice, his wife was at home with Scott. After Alfgar had gone to sleep, Alice had sent Bertha upstairs to bed at about nine o'clock. There was no one else with them after that, she maintained.

Another time, Bertha saw them in the bedroom. 'It was only on one occasion,' she said, 'at about eleven in the morning. Mr Thompson wasn't in the house.' She did not know how long they were there.

Another servant, Emma Burnett, was living on Parker Road with the Thompson family when Scott arrived. Emma remembered William went away for a week late in 1891, and said Mrs Thompson would see Scott during that time. She saw them walking together, alone but for Alfgar.

She was also shown the chemises Scott had claimed his mother had left behind. 'I wear them for softness next to my skin,' he told the police. 'She left them to me when she was here.' Emma shook her head at that statement. She had 'no doubt' they belonged to Alice.

Neighbours also saw compromising behaviour. People were easily shocked then. William Carter said he was startled once to see Scott take a bite from a slice of bread and jam and hand it to Alice to finish. 'I did not think that right between a man's wife and a single man.'

'Did you consider what you saw wrong and improper?' asked the Crown's lawyer.

'I did,' Carter declared.

Another time he saw them sitting by the fire, their chairs close enough for her feet to be nestling atop Scott's. As such intimate moments accumulated, so did his disapproval.

Mrs Carter said she'd seen Scott and Alice together outside – mostly in the orchard. She'd spotted them once sitting down by the creek. 'They just rose as I was coming,' she recalled. She noted that because the ground was mostly covered with tea-tree scrub, they couldn't be seen from Thompson's house.

However, no suspicions seemed to filter through to Thompson. On 8 October 1892, just three weeks before he died, he wrote to his mother in England to tell her she had another grandson and also to praise his good friend, Alex Scott.

> Dear Mother
>
> A few lines to say that we have another little son. He arrived on the 19th of September, and both are doing well. I did not get the news until four days after, so it was quite a surprise and a great weight off my mind. I am sorry to say I have not been in town to see them for a fortnight. I was taken bad on the 26th, and have been laid up ever since. I don't know what I should have done without the help of my neighbour Scott. He has been with me all the time and nursed me almost like a woman.

It was congestion of the liver, I think, and has been running on for a long time. I remember you used to suffer with yours once. What did you generally find best for it? I am very thankful to say I feel better again, and hope to pick up my strength again and get to work once more. Besides, I expect my little family will be home again soon, it will seem very different when they are back once more.

Somehow while lying sick I thought of bygone days, as I don't remember being in bed so long since the 'shingles', at Burton. It made me think at times I was back again and a boy at home. Ah well! The other land is nearer to us all than many think.

My love to you all,

Your loving son, William.

THE LETTER DID NOT REACH his mother, or at least not when it should have done. Just after William's death, Alice handed it to her friend John Herrold. He told the coroner that the tragedy had 'quite capsized' his mind, but he remembered Alice saying she'd been given it to post – presumably by Scott on one of his visits after Eric's birth. The letter should soon have been aboard a ship heading for England, but Alice had failed to mail it.

She didn't want the police to have it, but Herrold handed it over – with her reluctant permission. If she had opened the letter, she might have been glad for the police to see it because William's gratitude to Scott was clear. But maybe she'd kept it sealed, nervous about what it might contain. Or, possibly, she was reluctant to reveal her carelessness.

POISONING ON PARKER ROAD

An 1892 sketch from the New Zealand Observer and Free Lance *showing people involved in the inquest – Scott at centre, surrounded by witnesses, lawyers and the jury foreman. Ladies wore hats. Gentlemen were all bewhiskered. Illustration: PapersPast.co.nz*

Ten other short, cheerful letters written by Scott to Alice the previous June hint at how close the pair were. She had kept them in her dressing case – a box in which a lady would keep small items needed for daily beauty care. There were also four photographs of Scott in there, and she handed them to a detective the morning after William died. The letters were read out to the inquest jury.

CHAPTER ELEVEN

Several months before William died, when Alice was about seven months pregnant, she took Alfgar with her to Thames in July of 1892 and stayed for more than a month with William's uncle and his family. John W Hall was an ardent collector and planter of native trees. Many of those trees still survive in a Thames park named the John William Hall Arboretum. He and William used to swap notes about their mutual interest in botany.

Letters from Scott came to Alice from Auckland every few days during her holiday. While only one of her replies has survived, it's obvious from the dates on his notes that she replied to him promptly. His ten letters seem little more than friendly jottings, though a judge would later ask, 'What husband would be happy to have a man writing to his wife twice a week?'

The greetings are formal ('Dear Mrs Thompson', he always began) but fondness shines through – especially when he mentions Alfgar. Did this bachelor in his thirties feel real affection for the small boy, or was he just buttering up his mother?

Every letter ends with 'kisses to baby'. When Alice has been gone two weeks he asks, 'Does baby ever talk about Sunnydale? Do you think you would like to come back? You have not the slightest idea how the house is without him. I miss him very much. I wish he were here to annoy me and dance Highland flings all day if he liked. I would gladly put up with it all.'

Scott mentions he's caring for a plant Alice left with him ('there are two more blossoms out') and tells how he, Thompson and Carter have been rehearsing for a concert. 'I can tell you my fingers were sore. The bones go very well with two violins; it only wants a banjo to join in.'

There are comments about the prevalence of coughs and colds. 'You will have to take care of baby and yourself,' he writes, 'as this is, I think, about the worst time of the year.' He was hating the constant rain and wrote, 'I wish the winter was over.'

He keeps taking flowers to Ōrātia Cemetery. 'I am going to the station tomorrow, and I will take some violets and put them on the grave.' One note says he has visited weekly. Obviously, Alaric was still on Alice's mind, and Scott made sure she knew he was still tending the small grave.

He was also buying her books from a shop called Upton's. He refers to *Juanita*. Maybe it was *Juan and Juanita*, a popular 1888 tale of two kidnapped children who escape their captors and find their way home to Mexico through many perils.

Scott also asked Upton's to send her copies of *King Solomon's Mines* and *Beatrice* by the then famous novelist, H. Rider Haggard.

There are domestic news snippets from Sunnydale – a dog called Snap has taken over the couch, the house is looking clean and tidy, the fowls are existing on turnips without Alfgar at home to feed them oats and wheat, and a white pigeon is 'still sleeping at the front door'.

Gradually Scott's messages to Alfgar grow more affectionate. 'Give baby some kisses for me and tell him I've got a box full, which I am keeping till he returns. Ask him what he has done with all the kisses he had in the cushion for Mama and Mr Scott. Tell him I think Snap has got them all. He usually has the cushion for a pillow. Be sure and take good care of yourself, with kind regards, believe me, yours sincerely, Bertie Scott.'

He uses this Bertie nickname often.

There are darker comments too. He sometimes calls Sunnydale the 'House of Desolation' and makes other disparaging remarks.

His first letter, sent just after Alice's boat departed for Thames, reports her husband had started for home. 'I don't think he will be extra cheerful tonight,' writes Scott. 'I think Sunnydale should, in future, be changed to The Hermitage and "the hermit" should be added to Mr Thompson's long list of titles.'

A few days later he finds Thompson at home 'engaged doing domestic duties, in other words washing up dishes. He did not seem burdened with grief.' Scott's unspoken message: *your husband is not missing you.*

He goes on about how quiet it was. 'Stillness reigned supreme, scarcely a sound to be heard – a very near approach to a graveyard. To make things worse, it rained all day. So we took an armchair each, and stayed in front of the fire.' William apparently liked afternoon naps. Scott comments: 'For a wonder, Mr Thompson did not get drowsy during the day, but he made up for it during the evening by going to sleep about half-past seven and waking up a little after ten. He put it down to the frost. You know he always blames something for making him drowsy.'

He could tell her more about the House of Desolation, writes Scott, 'but I don't think it would be wise; I might get into trouble.'

In the next letter he says, 'I know you don't care about hearing news about Waikomiti people,' but then tells her about neighbours who are ill with influenza.

These little comments tell the story of complaints shared between two discontented people. Here was Scott, a long way from home but caring little. One of his letters mentions a brother's wedding in Australia. He declares he's not interested and, in fact, is glad to be clear of it.

And here was lonely Alice, stuck on a raw orchard far from the comforts of her old family home, with a husband who mostly liked solitude except when he took up his violin. It was perhaps no wonder they slept apart. Witnesses at various court hearings spoke of how Alice had said she wished William would return to lawyering in town, and of how she yearned for more company. If he was happy with rural life, it seems she certainly was not.

ALICE'S PREGNANCY was well advanced when Scott was writing that string of letters, but her condition is never mentioned. Looking back now, the huge unanswered question is: whose baby was it? If Alice and Scott became close in late 1891, then the baby expected in September of 1892 could have been fathered by him.

Just one short note from Alice to Scott was read out during legal hearings. It was written just before she returned home from

Thames in mid-July. It asks if he might meet her boat. 'I should like you to so much,' she says, 'if you don't think it too much trouble.'

Alice says Thompson can also do it, but she clearly wants Scott to be waiting for her at the wharf: 'I shall be so glad,' she repeats, ending with: 'Hoping to see you on Saturday, with lots of kisses from Alfgar and yours very sincerely, Alice Thompson.'

The police had found one other more business-like note written to Scott about posting something to him. She signed that one, 'Yours, D.'

Why the initial 'D'? And why the 'Bertie' name Scott often used for his sign-offs?

Those questions became much more acute when, on the day after William's death, the police opened an undated note they found in a pocket of Scott's trousers. It would become notorious as 'the Bertie Letter' and was avidly read by all of Auckland in the daily papers.

> Friday night.
>
> My Own Darling Wife,
>
> As I told you, T. went to town to-day, and has not yet returned. You can see by the notepaper where I am writing this. I am sitting down in my darling's chair to write. T said if he were not at home early would I come down and feed Rose [a cow] and Bess [one of William's horses], and I said I would; so am here waiting for him.
>
> Oh, my darling, what opportunities I am getting. I can do it any time, dear. I wish to God it was done so that I could call you my

very own. Oh, Dolly dear, what a difference between this Friday and last. Ah, my sweet wife. I was happy with you, darling. Are we going to have any more happy days? Dolly, my sweet wife, do you want to come back to your own Bertie? Do you, darling?

I am only just scribbling a few lines. I saw paper on the table. My Dolly, I won't wait much longer. I can't stand it.

Your own true, loving, and devoted husband, Bertie. I think I am writing with your pen; what do you think?

Bertie

THE LETTER WOULD BE DISSECTED MINUTELY by lawyers in the weeks ahead. They would also argue over whether the trousers that contained the letter were actually Scott's. Whether the handwriting matched that in his other letters. Whether the words 'wife' and 'darling' referred to Alice, as Scott might already have had some unknown wife. Whether Alice had ever received the note. There was no proof it had been posted to her – but also none that she had not seen it. The police pointed out that the paper, watermarked 'Original Turkey Mill, Kent', was identical to paper found in the Thompson house. It was a high-quality brand not found in every home.

People would deduce that 'T' stood for Thompson and 'D' was short for Dolly, Scott's pet name for Alice, which he'd once revealed to a neighbour. Most of all, gossip had to have circled around the desperation to call her 'his very own'.

The note made it easy for people to see him as guilty. It's also easy to imagine rumours that she knew of his intentions, and possibly even egged him on. Scott must have kicked himself for keeping it. And whether or not Alice had seen it before, she'd have been appalled when the letter came to light. And very afraid.

Carolyn and I mused about how much Alice knew. Had she been supporting Scott's scheme to do away with William? Or, tucked away at Helen Saul's house as she waited for her baby to come, did she have no idea what was going on at home?

No telephones on Parker Road, remember. And if Alice wasn't close to her neighbours, it's unlikely they would have written to her about her husband's failing health. Apparently she had no visitors except for Scott, who brought flowers from her garden but may have said nothing of William's vomiting bouts in the last month of his life.

We could understand how vulnerable Alice would have been to an attentive stranger. Having lost her first-born, she still had her second son but was mired in a difficult marriage. Her future must have felt bleak – stuck on a dreary orchard with a husband who was determined to stay up in the lonely hills, far from the livelier life she longed for.

'I think Scott was a shoulder to cry on,' Carolyn said. Yes. And no doubt flattered and charmed, Alice stepped into an affair.

CHAPTER TWELVE

The inquest that began at the Thompson house just after his death continued a week later at the New Lynn Hotel, a popular pub run by a woman licensee. It had a decent reputation and, even better, it was a much faster cab ride for Aucklanders than the long trip out to Sunnydale.

Five lawyers were involved by then, and three doctors. Two of the medical men were there to hear Roberton's descriptions of William's symptoms and give their own opinions on what might have caused them. No doctor – including Roberton – saw William at all before he died. Scott was also there every day, scribbling copious notes for his counsel, Samuel Hesketh.

An amused *Observer* writer noted that two of the medics eased their boredom taking secret photos of other people. You could already do that in the 1890s. One camera was like a metal disc on a neck string that could nestle under a man's waistcoat with the lens in a buttonhole.

Dr Haines sneakily snapped the coroner, who 'was so innocent of it all', wrote the reporter.

Those photos haven't survived, but newspaper artists' sketches hint at how people looked. There's Scott scribbling notes, a frown on his brow beneath a flopping curl of hair. His moustache extends in points, perhaps waxed for effect. His white-bearded uncle John Wilson wears a bowler hat and leans on a cane. Women in the witness box wear their best hats. The brims are tip-tilted, adorned with feathers and ribbons.

For five more days the inquest ground on. Finally, on 25 November, the six jury members retired to consider their verdict. After just an hour up stood the foreman. 'We find that the accused, Alexander James Scott, wilfully murdered the deceased, William Thompson, by administering strychnine poison.'

Guilty! And so swiftly. It wasn't even a month after William's death and already that dire word had emerged.

An unnamed *New Zealand Herald* editorial writer was outraged by how Scott had been found guilty so soon after William Thompson's death, as the verdict prejudiced proceedings that were still to come.

'Here is a verdict of guilty of murder actually recorded before trial, under the system of criminal investigation which boasts that its proudest feature is that the accused gets every possible advantage,' he wrote. This was farcical, he thundered, urging that the criminal system be reformed.

It would be 1908, however, before coroner's juries became optional and 1951 before they were abolished.

This six-man jury could even have got by with a majority verdict of only four, but their vote was unanimous. It probably wasn't surprising, given that Scott's own uncle had worried about his nephew's poison purchases. The *Auckland Star* reported Wilson as saying, 'I should not trust him with poison of any kind.'

A follow-up hearing at the magistrates' court then began on 9 December to assess if there was enough evidence for the case to go to the Supreme Court. The magistrate decided there was.

Back went Scott to a cell in Mt Eden Prison. He would have to wait three months for his Supreme Court date.

The prison was a grim place made of dark basalt stone. It's empty now, closed down since 2011, but life there was awful. In 1892 it was still only half-built, with convicts forced to work at building stone walls to replace an earlier timber stockade. Its grim front wall was complete when Scott went inside.

A friend of mine spent a few months there twenty years ago on a fraud charge. He is now successful in business and devoted to his family, but he is still haunted by the memory of the 'big iron-clad door' clanging behind him. 'I can sum up how it felt in one word. *Alone*. You are totally alone. Alone on an island in a castle locked up in the tower,' he told me. 'No friends, no family, nobody you can trust. If you are dependent, you are screwed. Meaning, dependent on family, friends, drugs, people, social contact, women or sex ... the list goes on. Alone, as in disconnected from the world you know.'

Meanwhile, Alice remained with her sons at Helen Saul's house. She probably stayed inside, away from sharp eyes and wagging tongues. News of the inquest's guilty verdict must have made her gut churn.

It's impossible to know if she and Scott wrote to each other then, or whether her love might have turned to loathing. There were strict rules about jail mail. Low-risk prisoners could send and receive only one letter a month and have one twenty-minute visit. Unruly or high-risk offenders might wait eight months to have any kind of contact with the world outside.* Alice would hardly have risked people learning she still had not given him up – if, in fact, that was the case.

There are hints, though, in the 'Bertie letter', that she had already pushed him away before William's death. Note the past tense: *I was happy with you, darling. Dolly, my sweet wife, do you want to come back to your own Bertie? Do you, darling?*

I *was* happy with you. It could indicate she'd already told him their affair was over and that note was Scott's desperate plea for her to return to him.

Out on Auckland's gentle slopes people talked, of course, about how Alice had stayed at the Thames home of William's uncle, who was a chemist. Might she have taken toxins from his shelves, or learnt useful tips about poisons she might have shared with Scott?

This idea was never mooted in the Supreme Court, but still, rumours would have floated over beer mugs and tea cups.

Sunnydale remained abandoned. Little Alfgar would no longer dance his Highland Flings there or get kisses from Scott. The man

---

* Mt Eden Gaol, nineteenth-century conditions, *Rock College: An unofficial history of Mount Eden Prison*, by Mark Derby, Massey University Press, 2020.

had disappeared forever from his life. Snap, the dog, was never mentioned again.

If the Sauls allowed Alice to stay on with them, she was either staying for free or somehow covering the expense herself. Many of William Thompson's bills had gone unpaid (as chemists and doctors would reveal at Scott's trial), but perhaps she had an allowance from her own family in England. Interestingly, Thompson's creditors seemed relaxed about those overdue bills. After all, he was a gentleman. He was *cultured*. Why, he had studied at Oxford!

One doctor was unconcerned about an outstanding two-year-old invoice. 'I haven't the slightest idea what his pecuniary position was,' he said in court. 'He [Thompson] owed me a bill, which has not been paid, but I had not the slightest doubt about his paying it.'

Whatever Alice's financial position, all she could do was wait and worry – because a tense meeting lay ahead with William's younger brother, twenty-seven-year-old Dr Charles Thompson. He was on his way to New Zealand to manage the family's interests on behalf of the grieving relatives back in Burton-on-Trent.

Archives of arriving ships' passenger lists are sketchy, and I could not find Charles's name in library records. Likely he arrived within three months of William's death. Once the trial began, he'd have avidly read the medical evidence. There'd have been a courtesy visit to Dr Roberton, too. Speaking doctor to doctor, they'd have been able to debate Scott's guilt or innocence with more know-how than the average juror.

PART II
CONSEQUENCES

CHAPTER THIRTEEN

Scott's Auckland Supreme Court trial began on 20 March 1893, nearly five months after Thompson's death. It would run for ten days, with forty witnesses called.

The Supreme Court had been built twenty-five years earlier in Gothic Revival style. The building's mellow brick walls, pointed archways, colonnades and gargoyles are still admired today, and it now serves as Auckland's High Court.

I was taken there once on a school trip. *Look, children, here are the basement cells where prisoners waited to be called. Here are the steps they climbed to the dock. Go up and look!*

It was creepy. The cell we saw was smelly and horrible, the stairs bleak and dirty, and the view from the dock intimidating. The courtroom had wood-panelled walls, rows of seats like church pews, and a judge's chair big enough for a king. I stood in that dock and looked around the gloomy chamber. Some sixty-five years earlier, Alexander Scott had stood there too.

His situation was unenviable. The six jurors at the inquest had already decided he was guilty of giving Thompson strychnine. All the intense press coverage would have meant the twelve-member Grand Jury knew that.

Day after day, he had to climb the steps to the dock to face the rows of avid stares. At that end of a humid Auckland summer, the court would have been hot and stuffy. No deodorants then. Imagine the sweat, stress and anxiety.

Spectators poured in. The *New Zealand Herald* noted the upper-level ladies' gallery was 'very well patronised'. Women were not allowed to step into the body of the court or to sit on a jury – that wouldn't happen for another fifty years. The graduation of New Zealand's first female lawyer, Ethel Benjamin, was still four years away. But this trial drew in 'ladies' in droves.

It was a spectacle – murder was a hanging offence.

The judge was Edward Tennyson Conolly, aged about seventy-one. He had a sterling background, having been minister of justice and attorney-general ten years earlier.

Then there were the lawyers. The Hesketh brothers, Scott's defence team, worked side by side. They'd come from Manchester – first Edwin and then Samuel.

Thirty years on, the Heskeths had both become eminent lawyers. Their name lives on in present-day Auckland commercial law firm Hesketh Henry. There are no Heskeths there now, but their name endures.

Opposing them were two tough prosecutors, Joseph Tole and Theo Cooper. Tole, by then aged forty-seven, had succeeded the judge as minister of justice when only in his mid-thirties. One of

Cooper's first jobs was as a lowly newspaper proofreader. A studious lad, he landed a job in a law office and by the age of thirty-three was a partner in his own firm.

So it was Joseph and Theo against Edwin and Samuel. At stake: the life of Alexander Scott. He arrived in court 'very neatly and carefully dressed, and evidently in the best of health', said the *Auckland Star*. He pleaded not guilty, but it did not take long for evidence against him to build.

THE FIRST WITNESS was laundress Emma Burnett. She'd already appeared at the inquest. The prosecution was keen to show Scott and Alice were close – and Emma knew things. She'd been working for the Thompsons when Alaric died in 1891 and told the court she was first aware of Scott at the end of that year.

Emma was able to identify a watch, chain, locket and ring as Alice's. Jurors would soon learn that Scott had pawned them. A second gold watch also came to light. Emma knew it, too, because inside its back was a photo of Alaric. She said the chemises found in Scott's room, which he'd claimed were his mother's, in fact belonged to Alice. 'One is marked S.A. on the corner,' she pointed out. Emma recognised the lace edging of the fabric and knew the stitched initials stood for Mrs Thompson's two first names, Sarah Alice.

An even younger woman was called that day. When Alice left home on 18 August to prepare for her baby's birth, she first lodged in Epsom with 'lady's nurse' Emily More.

No one at the trial asked why Alice had left home a full month before her baby was due, but childbirth was dangerous then.* Perhaps Alfgar's arrival had been difficult and Alice wanted expert help close by if her next labour was hard. Or perhaps she and William were just not getting on.

Mrs More apparently went out often, leaving behind her daughter, Amy, aged twelve. 'I know the prisoner by sight,' Amy piped up from the witness box. 'I have seen him at my mother's house very often during the time Mrs Thompson was there.' Children can be such keen observers. I imagine Scott staring at Amy from the dock, trying to remember if he'd even noticed her during his visits to Alice the previous August.

Amy would sometimes have to mind her little sister and Alfgar while the adults went into Alice's bedroom. 'They shut the door,' she said. 'Sometimes they stayed in the bedroom only a little while, at other times a good time.' Scott brought Alice fruit, cakes and flowers.

Meanwhile, William was still fit and healthy, probably amusing himself with his violin and missing his small family, quite unaware that his now very pregnant Alice was seeing Scott almost every day.

Samuel Hesketh was eager for more detail. How many times did Scott visit, he asked Amy. He probably wanted the number to be low but Amy said 'very often'. And every time there were those

---

* Maternal deaths in New Zealand, 1890, https://www3.stats.govt.nz/historic_publications/1890-official-handbook/1890-official-handbook.html#idsec t2_1_10579 In 1890, when white-settler population was about 625,000, ninety-nine women died in childbirth or of associated puerperal fever. (Māori births and deaths weren't even registered until 1925.) Now, when New Zealand's population is more than five million, there's an average of ten maternal deaths per year. If the 1890 rate still applied, that would be nearly eight hundred today.

private spells in the bedroom. Alice apparently soon told Mrs More she felt lonely there and stayed for only two weeks before moving on to Helen Saul's house, away from Amy's gaze.

SCOTT'S UNCLE John Wilson was also in the witness box that day, talking about his worries over Scott's poison-shopping. He also spoke of how Scott had pleaded guilty in 1891 to a charge of obtaining money under false pretences. Wilson had tried to help then by telling the court his nephew had a 'weakness of the mind' and there was 'no reason at all' for what he'd done. Scott's mother in Australia had written a letter pleading for leniency then. It worked: Scott got just six months of probation, partly because his small crime had scored him a meagre seven shillings and sixpence. Conolly had been the judge that day too, on 10 March 1891, exactly two years before the start of the murder trial.

Now, with his nephew's life at stake, Wilson revealed he had been 'appointed to look after Scott for his father'. It seems Scott wasn't in Auckland just for fun or to help out on Wilson's farm. He was a problem son.

Wilson said Scott always had money to go into town and return with. That way, 'he would have no temptation to do anything that was wrong'. He handed his own cash to Scott, hoping it would stop him cheating or stealing from anyone else.

Today, an accused's previous record can't be raised in court. It prevents juries being influenced by earlier crimes. In Scott's case, though, not only was he on trial for a murder he'd already been found guilty of, but the fraud story showed he couldn't be trusted with money, let alone his best friend's wife. Right away his case was compromised.

The fifth witness that day was a William Powell. Once a respected chemist, he wasn't called at the Thompson inquest for he had himself been on trial at the time for providing abortions. This was a very serious crime. Now he and Scott were inmates of the same prison.

Detective Chrystal, who in early November had discovered Alice Thompson's birth-control device, was at Powell's place just a few days later, looking for different evidence of wrongdoing related to women. In a bedroom drawer he found forceps, a speculum, a catheter and some thin flexible sticks. The *Star* reported these 'were said to have been used by Samoans and Fijians to procure abortions'.*

POWELL'S TRIAL had featured many of the men now involved in the Scott trial. The same Joseph Tole who was now prosecuting Scott had had the same job when Powell was in the dock. Tole had also represented the Crown at the inquest into Thompson's death. Powell's defence lawyer had been Edwin Hesketh, who was now defending Scott alongside his brother, Samuel. He'd also earlier acted for Scott over the business of the forged cheque.

Such a small world it was, in this little city at the end of the empire. Everyone in the law knew everybody else. It was an even

---

* Sticks used to bring about miscarriage – bougies. On Britain's Science Museum website is a slender rod labelled 'urethral bougie made of wood with rounded ends, from Fiji, 1822–1930'. https://collection.sciencemuseumgroup.org.uk/objects/co107349/urethral-bougie-made-of-wood-with-tapering-rounded-bougies smaller world in prison, with Powell and Scott behind bars at the same time.

Powell's trial was about his effort to end the pregnancy of a ship's stewardess, who nearly died afterwards of an infection. Jurymen were probably puzzled by the speculum Detective Chrystal had found in Powell's room. They were unlikely to have seen one before. Inserted into the vagina and then levered open, its purpose is to provide a clear view of the cervix. Modern versions are still used today, but the speculum has a horrible history. It was invented in the 1840s by an American doctor, James Sims,* who used to try it out on female slaves he kept in a compound behind his private hospital.

Though Powell swore that he'd only ever used his drawer full of instruments for midwifery purposes, he had been convicted and hit with a ten-year sentence. Now he was back in court to say he'd supplied Scott with six grains of strychnine. Why? 'For poisoning cats that had been killing his chickens,' he said. The name Scott wrote in the poisons book was Edward Williams. Powell added it was only when the two men saw each other behind bars that he learnt Scott's true name.

Next up, a warder told the court how he'd processed Scott on his arrival in jail and found a watch in his coat pocket. A city watchmaker then testified William Thompson had once brought in the same watch for repair. 'I know it from the number and from the name.'

All eyes must have turned to Scott then. This was shocking, for the jurors were aware that when William wrote to his mother he'd

---

* Sims' history, https://www.history.com/news/the-father-of-modern-gynecology-performed-shocking-experiments-on-slaves

warmly described Scott as his friend. So how had William's timepiece made its way into Scott's pocket? Had he stolen it from dead (or nearly dead) William on the night of his death?

CHAPTER FOURTEEN

The next day the court was crowded again. The first witness was a pawnbroker, who said Scott had come twice in July of 1892 to pawn Alice's ring, a gold chain and a lady's gold watch. There was no mention of how much cash he had been able to raise. Alice was away in Thames that month. Did she know what Scott was doing with her jewellery? Did she miss it when she came home? It seems nobody asked her.

Then Bertha Kennerley gave evidence again. The young washerwoman had worked at Sunnydale every two weeks in Alice's absence. She remembered a time before Thompson died when she did not see him, but Scott had told her he was sick. On the following washday she'd heard him vomiting in the bedroom. On her next visit he trudged out of his room with a blanket around his shoulders. He was on his own and said Scott was 'away on horseback somewhere'. Thompson was always cheerful, she said, and had told her – laughing as he said it – that he 'had no use in his hands and feet. He said his legs were like wooden legs.'

Next on the stand was Dr McKellar, Alice's doctor.

Prosecutor Tole wanted to know whether Scott was visiting Alice soon after the birth. Women with sufficient time and money usually convalesced for about two weeks then. McKellar didn't know Scott was turning up at her bedside. 'I would not have allowed him to visit her personally during those fourteen days when she was not out of her bed,' he declared.

Was his stance due to 'motives of propriety or by reason of her health', asked the judge. Both, said the doctor.

Then Helen Saul testified that Scott had been a regular visitor after baby Eric's birth, usually bringing flowers from Sunnydale. 'On the fourth day he saw her in her bedroom.' He didn't stay long, visited her again while she was still in bed, and kept on coming twice a week.

Today's new mothers are usually up and about soon after delivery, so it's striking to read it was fifteen or sixteen days after Eric's arrival before Alice was able to take 'walking exercise'.

First she ventured onto the veranda, then graduated to short walks and became more active as October wore on. On the 27th, she enjoyed a leisurely four-hour drive out to St Johns in east Auckland with Mr and Mrs Saul. I think of them sitting up in a buggy, enjoying the view, being drawn along by a horse harnessed up with gleaming leather. Maybe the sight and sounds of the ride reminded Alice of her father's busy horse-tack factory back in Walsall. By October's end, the doctor said, she'd been capable of driving out to Waikomiti 'without danger'.

Then came the odd events of Saturday the 29th, which was when (according to Mrs Saul) Alice had intended to go home. She'd been absent from Sunnydale for ten weeks by then. But Scott came to see her that morning. They talked. And suddenly she wasn't leaving at all. Why the change of plan? Helen Saul did not know. The next time she saw Scott it was Monday morning, and he and Dr McKellar were on the doorstep with news of William's death.

Other witnesses on day two included more chemists. In July and August, Scott had ridden around town buying items ranging from toothache powder to arsenic, laudanum, prussic acid and strychnine. Chemist David Orr was instructed to send his bill to the Thompsons. This was apparently a normal kind of arrangement. Scott told Orr his name was Charles Gordon and he wanted strychnine crystals to poison dogs. Earlier, he'd fed Powell a tale about cat-killing.

Orr found him to be as normal as the next man. 'All his senses were quite sound. There were no symptoms of insanity as far as I could see.'

On day three, William Thompson's neighbour, Carter, was called to repeat his stories of telltale familiarity between Scott and Alice. In cross-examination, he was asked if he'd suggested to Thompson that Scott might be poisoning him. Yes, said Carter. But Thompson saw 'no reason' why Scott should harm him.

Carter didn't say if Alice's name came into that conversation, but it seems it was easier to suggest poisoning than to hint that Alice might be unfaithful. So William didn't hear about the bread-and-jam moment. Nor did Carter tell him of the nestling of feet in front of the fireplace – even though he said in court he 'did not think that was right between a man's wife and a single man'.

'Did you consider what you saw wrong and improper?' Hesketh asked.

'I did,' said Carter.

Wasn't it his duty as Thompson's friend, pressed the defence lawyer, to tell him about it?

'Not my business,' Carter replied.

Hesketh was hoping the jury would understand how hidden doubts might have been driving William to suicidal despair. 'During his illness, did Mr Thompson appear to have some trouble on his mind?'

'Once or twice,' said Carter.

Hesketh circled back to previous testimony: 'Now, did you not say when Mr Thompson was playing the violin, it seemed as if something was troubling him?'

'I believe I did.'

It makes me feel for William. I can see him drawing his violin bow across the strings as he sat alone next to his five hundred trees, and descending into depression despite the happy face he showed to his neighbours.

NEXT DAY, the *Herald* reported the prisoner still appeared to be in excellent health. 'His spirits seemed to be wonderfully good. He spent a considerable amount of time in writing.'

Conolly was tetchy, ordering one man to 'speak up!' and scoffing at his excuse that he had toothache. When another mumbler took the stand, Conolly growled, 'If this witness is going to stand up and gabble away in a tone that no one can hear, he may just as well go home again.'

Samuel Hesketh got into trouble by asking Eliza Carter what had happened to the candle the neighbours used when they listed the contents of William's room. 'Do you really mean to tell me,' snapped the judge, 'that exactly what was done with this candle is of importance?'

'Yes,' Hesketh insisted.

'I say it is *rubbish*,' said Conolly. It was not mentioned again.

CHAPTER FIFTEEN

Then Dr Roberton took the stand. He said Scott had visited several times in October to say his friend Thompson needed medicine. On 11 October, there were stories of bouts of vomiting, weakness and fever – once in late September and then again later on. It was continuing, said Scott. He added Thompson was taking Eno's fruit salts and calomel pills.

Eno's had been popular for easing poor digestion since the 1850s. Invented by British pharmacist James Eno, it claimed to drive out 'disease germs' and was good for 'biliousness, sick headache and errors in diet'. Combining baking soda, salt and citric acid, it is now known as Eno and is still on supermarket shelves.

Calomel was another old-time remedy used as a laxative. According to the doctor, Scott said William had pains in the stomach, chiefly after vomiting, but that 'the most pain was all over him'.

Roberton had concluded there was 'some irritation in the stomach' and prescribed a soothing mixture. Scott also asked for quinine for fever, adding the rather odd comment that William 'liked his medicine bitter'. Roberton said it should be taken only if William was feverish, as it could upset his stomach again. A prescription was produced for the judge to see. 'I suppose it is couched in the usual unintelligible terms,' he complained.

The doctor had given Scott a note for William with instructions that he wanted an update on the patient in a few days. Back at Sunnydale, Scott had told a neighbour about the note but didn't show it to him, saying the GP had seen no need at all to lay eyes on the patient. Scott did return to Roberton two days later to report the patient was 'ever so much better', though very weak, but now had a sore throat and a cold. This time the need was for a throat gargle and the doctor had duly prescribed one. He also gave Scott another note for William. It warned that failing to take care of himself could risk an attack of peritonitis or inflammation of the stomach. He should 'take milk and avoid cold'.

This arms-length kind of doctoring would be unthinkable today. But back then, if you lived out of town and had no telephone, haphazard prescribing was common. There seems to have been more trust in that era, too. You relied on neighbours to look after you in hard times.

Scott came to Roberton a few more times, always alone. He kept saying his friend was better but still rather weak. And then, finally, came that dead-of-night visit at October's end when Scott announced Thompson was dying – and that he might have taken strychnine.

So, what proof was there that William Thompson was suicidal? It was only Scott who pushed the idea. Of course, fatherly grief was natural after the death of baby Alaric, said Dr McKellar. Moorhead testified that William had 'fretted' for about a month but got reconciled to his loss. Alaric had been terribly ill, suffering so much that Thompson said he was 'rather more pleased than otherwise that the child died'.

Neighbour James Parker said while Thompson could be hasty and eccentric, he was usually cheerful. His favourite expression was: 'I like this life, and feel as jolly as a sand-boy.' Thompson was always 'ready to crack a joke at any time', said William Carter. And a nurseryman who knew him testified as to his 'very jolly disposition'.

Helen Saul concurred that Thompson was 'cheerful'. She described Scott as 'eccentric', adding he had 'a rather wild, excited manner'. Carter said Thompson did not seem likely to take his own life, but he had 'no doubt he had trouble on his mind'.

So, here was Thompson, whose farm was struggling, who was short of money, whose first child had died horribly, who for many weeks had hardly seen his wife and second son and had held his newborn infant only once.

Maybe he suspected Alice no longer loved him. He might have been longing for her to return but also dreading it, for if their marriage was broken it needed re-mending. But how? No one did relationship counselling in the nineteenth century except perhaps for churchmen, whose chief role was probably to tell unhappy spouses to remember their marriage vows.

On the other hand, if a man is planning on poisoning himself, would he do it in a slow, miserable kind of way that causes repeated vomiting for a month before finally his body gives out? It seems unlikely. You'd surely want your fatal dose to be large, failure-proof and final, not drawn out in tiny unpleasant increments like some slow form of torture.

And what of that little phial of strychnine that Dr Roberton found by Thompson's bed? At the trial, he said the crystals inside it were very bitter to the taste. 'I said so to Scott,' he told the court. 'I remarked that it might be either strychnine or quinine.'

WHAT IS it like to die of strychnine poisoning? Terrible. Victims endure waves of convulsions that turn muscles rigid and force the spine back into an excruciating arch. The pain can go on for hours.

Jane Stanford, one of the co-founders of California's Stanford University, was murdered by strychnine in 1905 while on holiday in Hawaii. Her passing was grim. With each convulsion her head strained back, her thighs stretched wide, her feet twisted in and her hands became immovable fists. As a doctor and servants struggled to help her, she managed to gasp in between terrible contractions, 'This is a horrible death to die!' Finally her breathing stopped as the toxin paralysed her lungs.*

So, given the extreme death throes suffered by strychnine victims, why was William Thompson's bedding smoothly draped over his body? Parker, who knew nothing of how he'd died except for Scott's fleeting mention of 'spasms', noted the odd state of the bed.

Before galloping off to Auckland, did Scott wait until William was gone and then straighten the covers before alerting the neigh-

---

* *Stanford* magazine story on Jane Stanford's mysterious death, https://stanfordmag.org/contents/who-killed-jane-stanford

bours? When all the time he knew there was no help to be found for the dead man?

CHAPTER SIXTEEN

Dr Roberton was asked at the trial for the time of death, but he had no sure way of knowing. All he could do was compare the cooling body with the temperature of his own hand.

Thermometers did exist then. The first portable mercury thermometer had been invented twenty-five years earlier, following earlier research by a clever German named Fahrenheit. The device took five minutes to produce a reading. Roberton didn't have one the night William died.

His examination was done by the flickering light of a single candle. He told the judge there was a table by the door with a soup plate and a basin of food on it, but the neighbours who'd earlier made their list of the room's contents did not notice that table at all.

Roberton found a glass containing mixed mustard and a spoon on a bedside chair, along with an oval dish. The crystal phial was revealed when he lifted the dish. The neighbours had not seen the shiny trinket either.

It was rather cold that night, the doctor said. It was somewhat warm, said another witness. There were so many differing opinions.

The jam dish, the spoon, the glass – none of them were sent to Mr Pond, the analyst, for closer examination. As I read about that I was thinking, *the jam, the jam!* If you were trying to disguise bitterness, wouldn't you cover it up with sugary jam? That's what my mother did when I was little and needed penicillin or sulfa for some infection or other. Pills weren't encapsulated in plastic then and were big and bitter.

I remember her nudging my lips with a teaspoon, its bowl brimming with honey or jam in which floated tiny white flecks of pills she'd crushed to make me better. Did Scott coax a lethal spoonful of jam into William's mouth in this way, or did William take it himself? Roberton said in court he had 'felt' jam in the spoon, presumably by testing with a finger.

He also said he had no doubts about the cause of death. Strychnine. Pointers included the 'extremely marked post-mortem rigidity of the body', stiff calves with toes 'pointing right out', and clenched hands. The post-mortem had shown no signs of death by natural causes.

'You have no doubt about the death being caused by strychnine?' pressed prosecution lawyer Tole.

'None,' said Roberton.

Justice Conolly wanted to know if William might have been conscious to the end.

Yes, said the doctor.

The judge, puzzling over the mystery of the smooth bedding, wanted to know if Thompson might have died during a paroxysm or in a quieter time in between spasms. But Roberton could not help: 'I have not been able to form an opinion.'

As for time of death, he said he thought it might have happened between seven and ten hours before he arrived at the death scene. The body's temperature was about the same as that of the room.

Justice Conolly was curious about Thompson's bouts of vomiting in the month before he died. 'Vomiting is not a symptom of strychnine poisoning?' he wanted to know.

'No,' said Roberton.

'It is of arsenical poisoning, is it not?'

'Yes.'

AH, arsenic, chief ingredient of the Rough on Rats that Scott had also been buying. Pond, the analyst, would soon tell the court he found no trace of arsenic in Thompson's body. It is tasteless and therefore easy to experiment with. So did Scott try it first in small doses to test its effects, only to be frustrated when it merely caused vomiting? And then, losing patience, did he give William a strychnine-laced spoonful of jam, relying on sugar to disguise the bitterness?

Or did despairing William do all of that to himself?

Another chemist stepped up then. John Jefferson spoke of Scott's many visits to his Symonds Street pharmacy during September, when he bought saccharine for sweetening, strychnine for killing cats that were attacking his chickens and, later, Rough on Rats to do the job when the cats failed to die. Scott's shopping list included morphia for sleeplessness and to ease a pain in his shoulder.

Scott also talked about his sick friend, Thompson, and asked for sarsaparilla, commonly used for joint pain and skin itching. Oh, and liniment, please, for the patient's back. Also, there was vomiting and 'severe diarrhoea'. Mr Jefferson gave him the sarsaparilla along with calomel pills for the digestive problems.

After about five of these visits, the chemist suggested that surely the ailing Mr Thompson needed a doctor. That, said Scott, would be too expensive.

Scott was back again on 1 October, wanting something for his own sleeping problem. He'd decided against more morphia and asked for chloral hydrate – a handy hypnotic drug that was good for insomnia.

Scott had to sign for it in the poisons book. He used a false name, Edward Wilson, for all these purchases. Jefferson was unconcerned by his many needs. 'He appeared to me to have a decided knowledge of medicines, and he appeared conversant with the properties of the poisons. I noticed no indication in him of weakness of mind and I did not hesitate to supply him with poisons.'

Jefferson was also content to comply with Scott's request that all his shopping be billed to William Thompson. Five months after Scott's final purchase, that account, too, was still unpaid.

A NOTHER OBSERVANT WOMAN was called next. Matilda Groves spoke of how, a few weeks before Thompson died, she had gone to his house on an errand. She asked Scott how William was. Getting better, she heard, but not so well that day. No doctor had been called. Thompson couldn't afford it, Scott told her.

'I recommended Dr Kenderdine, who generally went to poor people for nothing,' said Mrs Groves. But Scott did not believe in doctors – he called them 'humbugs'. This was Victorian slang for people who were insincere or deceptive. And Thompson wouldn't see Kenderdine anyway, said Scott, 'because he was not the family doctor'.

Matilda told the court she'd seen Scott and Mrs Thompson out together, often with Alfgar. 'Sometimes Scott would say to me he was going to see "his girl" and at other times he said he was going to see "Dolly" at the waterfall.' Who was Dolly, she wanted to know. 'He said it was Mrs Thompson.'

I was curious to see the waterfall, so Carolyn took me there one day. It's about a ten-minute stroll from the house that used to be Sunnydale, with bushy glades and grassy fields in between. Because of dry weather the waterfall was more of a stepped stream on that summer day, tumbling over rocks in a narrow, fern-filled gully. It's quiet there. Beautiful. Secluded. A perfect meeting place for lovers.

Mrs Groves thought Scott had arrived on Parker Road in December of 1891. 'I had many conversations with him. He always seemed very nice to me.'

Cross-examined by Edwin Hesketh, she described how Scott had once dropped by when she was milking a cow. And as she worked, he read out loud a letter signed by someone named Dolly. Hesketh did not ask what 'Dolly' had written.

James Martin, the Parnell livery stables owner, was up next. He said Scott had arrived at his premises the day before Thompson died, riding Alice's own chestnut horse. Martin did not say what time of day it was.

Scott said he was in town to get medicine for Mr Thompson, who was very ill. He'd pushed the horse hard and wanted a fresh one so he could return quickly. Scott also asked Martin to send a cab to pick up Mrs Thompson that afternoon at Mrs Saul's so she could go out and do some shopping. As usual, he asked for the fees to be put on the Thompson account.

Away he went. But instead of rushing back to the patient, did he instead detour to Alice's door and persuade her to delay returning home? Perhaps he used the afternoon cab ride as a ruse to ensure she would stay put. One of Martin's cab drivers said from the witness box that he went to Mrs Saul's as ordered, picked up the two women plus Alice's boys and spent two hours driving them around Auckland shops. Maybe Alice saw it as a last pleasurable outing before returning to the 'House of Desolation'.

Another Waikomiti neighbour said Scott had told her Alice's doctor advised she was too weak to come home yet. This was a week before Thompson died, but Dr McKellar would say something quite different later in court about her health at that time. He pronounced her quite fit to travel by then.

CHAPTER SEVENTEEN

Day five arrived. Enter James Pond, a fellow of the Society of Public Analysts, London. Three days after the autopsy, the police had brought him a small silver-capped crystal phial and some wide-mouthed bottles containing portions of William's body. One held his stomach and its contents, the second had bits of liver, spleen and kidneys, and the third, parts of the large intestine.

As I read about that, I wondered how well preserved the specimens might have been. Ice was available in Auckland then. There had been an 'Ice, Aerated Water, and Ginger Beer Factory' in the city for ten years. It made ice with a machine that used ether as a refrigerant.

None of the trial reports mention if the police station had a way to keep evidence chilled. The jars were possibly stored in an ice box. If so, it was maybe not very efficient. By the time Pond got to work, the cork on the jar containing stomach tissues had burst and a portion of stomach wall was poking out.

The cork was tied down with a fastening of gutta-percha. Like rubber, it's a sap extracted from trees in tropical Asian rainforests. But unlike rubber, it is mouldable when warmed and re-hardens when it cools. It was regarded as wonderful stuff then, with many uses, from sheathing submarine telegraph cables and filling dental cavities to making golf balls and knife handles.

However, gutta-percha and cork were no match for William's stomach contents, though Pond must still have had enough to work with. When he examined an ounce and a half of tissue he found 'food contents that were faintly acid, reddish brown in colour, containing a small amount of pulpy matter'. He concluded it was jam.

Pond then described the gruesome and fiddly process of finely mincing and distilling tissues in a search for poison. From what he had on hand he obtained 'not less than one third of a grain of strychnine'. He found no sign of arsenic or any other poison.

So, what is a 'grain' of strychnine? Medicines are measured in milligrams now, but yesterday's apothecaries (pharmacists) saw things more literally. A grain stood for an actual grain, as in the tiny seeds of cereal plants like wheat and barley. Today, one grain converts to 64.79mg.

How much strychnine can kill a person? A chemical safety information group called Inchem[*] puts it at 30–120mg. Agonising seizures begin after it's swallowed, leading eventually to asphyxia. Death might occur after several hours of extreme pain, though when Jane Stanford was stricken in her luxury Honolulu hotel, it was all over in fifteen or twenty minutes. You can't buy strychnine

---

[*] Strychnine lethality, www.inchem.org

over a chemist's counter today, but it's still used in some pesticides, particularly as a rat killer.

Pond told the judge that if he'd had all of the liver, spleen and kidneys on hand he would have found 'not less than a grain of strychnine'. In other words, a dose of 64.79mg – well capable of killing William.

Justice Conolly wished more of the body had been tested. 'This evidence is rather vague,' he complained. But it was enough. If Pond estimated he would have found a grain, and a grain could kill a man, then that was that.

INSPECTOR BROHAM WAS UP NEXT. He was only there to say he'd delivered the jars of body tissues to Pond. But defence lawyer Hesketh brought up the tiny crystal phial and its fragments of strychnine crystals. Had the inspector interviewed Alice Thompson, asked Hesketh? Yes, said Broham, on the morning when she viewed her husband's body. And could he trace the phial to the deceased?

'Well, Mrs Thompson made a statement to me with regard to that phial.'

The *Auckland Star* recorded that Mr Hesketh 'pressed the question', but the judge raised his hand. He did not want to hear second-hand evidence. 'She has chosen to leave the country,' he said. 'It could at the best be only hearsay evidence.'

This was the first time the court heard that Alice was no longer even in New Zealand. She had left a month before the trial began, and, if the judge was to be believed, had gone of her own volition.

If you were an onlooker avid to lay eyes on her, you were sorely disappointed.

Scott must have known she had sailed away – his lawyers would have told him. I imagine his heart sinking when he realised he wouldn't see her again. He may have been bitter. Or he may have been glad. She had been the cause and centrepiece of his adoration. She was free now. He was not. Now he could only watch as Hesketh bored on. 'Have you any doubt that if you had placed Mrs Thompson in the witness box she would have traced that phial to the deceased?' Hesketh was eager to prove it was William's, for that gleaming little tube with its lethal toxic fragments could add weight to the suicide theory.

The policeman wasn't about to give Hesketh that satisfaction. 'I have every doubt,' he said. He gave nothing else away.

Oh, the frustration for Hesketh as he asked what Alice might have said in earlier court hearings – if she'd been called to appear.

'She was not called,' said the inspector.

'Why not?'

'That rested entirely with the Crown prosecutor.'

Perhaps she wasn't brought to court because she could have linked the phial to her husband. 'Was not this the reason?' Hesketh asked the inspector.

Broham hedged again, saying he'd not been in charge of the case after he'd arrested Scott. In other words: *nothing to do with me.*

Detective Grace was next. He said he'd stood on the wharf on 16 February and watched as Alice Thompson boarded the *Aorangi*. It steamed off for distant England at 4pm.

Tole, the prosecutor, had a question for him. 'Did you know that on that day, or the day previous, she had been subpoena'd by Mr Hesketh?'

'Yes,' Grace said.

'Why were you on the wharf when Mrs Thompson left?'

'I was there to prevent her going, if Mr Hesketh desired it.'

Justice Conolly was dismissive. 'I don't see how you were going to prevent her going. Neither the Crown nor the prisoner could have detained her. I don't see how anyone could have kept her here against her will.' No one was wanting to get her away, he added.

By 'no one' he no doubt meant forces of the law. But Dr Charles Thompson was in New Zealand by then and he could have been eager for his sister-in-law to vanish. Someone would have had to arrange her passage home. Maybe he did. He wouldn't have relished his late brother's unfaithful wife making a spectacle of herself in a murder trial. It is also possible, of course, that he had kinder motives in helping her get away unscathed. He might have seen her as a foolish and naïve woman who'd been taken in by a scoundrel. Or perhaps he just wanted her gone.

It's a puzzle, though, that she apparently went without her sons. Maybe her anxiety was so high by then that Charles did not trust her with their care on the long voyage. He'd have promised his family to carry them safely to Burton-on-Trent. The boys were Thompsons, after all, his dead brother's sons. They were precious. Perhaps she was persuaded to go solo, broken-hearted or not, though baby Eric was only five months old and Alfgar's fourth birthday was just eight days away.

Alice would have been shattered after all that'd happened. Getting ready to travel is always stressful and she also had to rid herself of Sunnydale, a.k.a. the House of Desolation. It was bought by a fireman named Peter Nightingale only three days before the *Aorangi* sailed. Selling under pressure, she may have had to let it go for a bargain price.

In fact, Hesketh ached to put Alice in the witness box but could not make her stay. When the trial was over, he wrote a letter to the editor of the *Star* to make sure everyone knew how she'd slipped away.

In preparing to defend Scott, he realised Alice had not appeared at any previous hearings. He also heard she'd made a statement to the police about the crystal phial and was planning to leave. A rumour was floating around town about what she might have said – and he wanted the jury to hear it.

But then he was surprised to discover he had no power to hold her in New Zealand at all. 'In the face of all I could do, she could leave if she were so determined.'

If she'd been a witness for the Crown at the inquest or the magistrates' court hearings, she would also have been legally bound to appear at the Supreme Court if the Crown wanted her there. But the prosecuting lawyers weren't interested. And the defence's desire for her presence meant nothing.

Three days before Alice was due to leave, he tried to convince the Crown team to call her but was ignored. If Tole had agreed, then Detective Grace could have stopped her boarding her ship. Hesketh was stymied. Under British law she could have been detained, but out in England's most distant colony the relevant act was not yet in the law books.

Hesketh still issued a subpoena, despite knowing it was pointless. It arrived only half an hour before Alice's departure time. How that must have shocked her.

Was she already standing on the wharf? Maybe Charles and Helen Saul were there, too, to see her off. Perhaps they urged her to ignore it – to just get on the ship and go. Her heart would have pounded as she climbed the gangplank. Imagine her relief as the *Aorangi*'s hawsers were unhitched and a widening gap opened between ship and dock.

Detective Grace's dockside vigil was no use at all other than to confirm Alice was gone. With her went any chance of disclosure about Scott's (and her own) behaviour, the wording of the infamous 'Bertie letter', her husband's state of mind, the mysterious phial, the tension in her marriage, their money problems – what she knew and what she didn't.

THE PROSECUTION CALLED several other witnesses that day. William Thompson's cousin, Ellen Hall of Thames, said that when Alice had stayed with her family in June and July of the previous year, she hadn't been short of cash and hadn't asked anyone in the house for a loan. That was the period in which Alice and Scott were writing cheerful notes to each other.

Detective Chrystal also described how the 'Bertie letter' had been found in Scott's trousers, and its scandalous contents were duly read out. The jury also heard about the preventative pessary.

Two prison warders and a nurseryman who knew the accused's handwriting were asked who they thought had penned the Bertie note. Scott, they said. Prosecuting lawyer Theo Cooper said he would also call an expert handwriting witness. Justice Conolly snorted. 'I may be peculiar, but I don't believe in experts' evidence in this matter.'

Handwriting had been much studied, argued Cooper. Why, there was a volume of two thousand pages in the library on the analysis of writing.

'I am sorry money has been wasted in such a way,' scoffed the judge. 'You and I, Mr Cooper, accustomed to seeing a good deal of correspondence, are as good experts as anyone else.'

CHAPTER EIGHTEEN

The trial ground on into Saturday too. Up next were two more doctors, Haines and Lewis. Neither of them had seen Thompson at all during his illness, but both concurred with the strychnine theory.

Hesketh grilled them on Thompson's earlier bouts of sickness more than a month before his death. What other kinds of irritants could have caused them? Someone suggested ptomaine poisoning (the common term then for food poisoning). Could William have eaten bad meat? Meat pies had recently poisoned six people in Parnell. Three of them had died.

The judge mentioned that Scott had sometimes pre-cooked meals for Thompson so he could reheat them later. There were no fridges in nineteenth-century cottages. As every modern food safety expert knows, leaving food tepid for hours and then rewarming it can easily make food go 'off' and bring about vomiting.

But then Justice Conolly checked his notes and saw that William mostly had broth and jellies in his final weeks. So, they could infer William was not taking solid food. Maybe it was tiredness or the heat, but as the day wore on the talk became quite silly. 'There was a fowl spoken of, Your Honour,' said Hesketh. Dr Haines said it was normal for prescriptions to contain poisons – 'They would prove fatal if enough of them were taken.'

Conolly: 'Some of the commonest domestic medicines would be fatal if you took enough of them.'

Cooper: 'A bottle of whisky contains a fatal dose.'

Hesketh: 'Even cold water would do harm if you drank enough of it.'

All of this was more than one jury member could stomach. Today, jury members' names are not revealed, but in 1893 the *Herald* was free to mention Charles Hooper Green, 'a stout middle-aged gentleman who certainly looked very far from being well' and 'threatened to collapse'. He suddenly announced he was too ill to go on. 'I scarcely know what to do with myself. I have had no rest at night, and I feel my feet getting so cold. Just let me out in the air for five minutes.'

It's hard now to believe a murder trial would continue with a juror so desperate to lie down, but Samuel Hesketh suggested a bed could be brought into court, as had happened at a previous trial.

'That would not do in my case, Your Honour,' said Green.

'Perhaps the whole of the jury had better go for a walk,' suggested the judge. Out they all went and soon Green returned, promising to persevere. Scott could only look on impatiently. Here he was with his life in the balance and this juryman was barely alert.

Tole wrapped up the case for the prosecution at 5pm that Saturday. Edwin Hesketh didn't want to open his case for the defence right then. It was late. He was very tired, and Monday was a much better option. Justice Conolly wanted to go on. 'We have had six days this week, and have done very little,' he grumbled. But when he asked the jury if they could continue for another hour, the foreman said no. They wanted to adjourn at once. And so the court did.

FOR SCOTT, the empty Sunday must have seemed endless. He'd have wondered about Alice all through the trial – where in the world she was and what she was thinking. She was by now tossing about on the Atlantic, approaching the coast of England

The voyage usually took five weeks, calling at Montevideo, Rio de Janeiro and Tenerife on the trip back to England around Cape Horn. I could not find any records for the date her ship left Auckland, so there's no passenger list on which she might have appeared. She would not have needed a passport when she boarded the *Aorangi* – they weren't introduced by either Britain or New Zealand until 1915. In the 1890s you simply bought a ticket and travelled. Might she have travelled under another name anyway? It would have been humiliating if other passengers knew she was *that woman* whose Australian lover who was on trial for her husband's murder.

What a long voyage it was. Early steamships heaved and pitched in rough seas. Passengers shivered in icy southern gales and sweltered in the blazing tropics.

An *Aorangi* shipboard diary from the 1890s,* kept by traveller Edith Goodman, records day after day of stultifying routine. Passengers passed the time with skipping and quoits when the weather allowed. Below decks they played the piano, read books and wrote letters; they played card games, dominoes and a popular board game called Reversi.

In bad weather it was hard to sleep. 'Woken during the night by crockery in the pantry being jerked off shelves and getting smashed,' wrote Mrs Goodman one morning. Stewards fixed frames around table edges in rough weather to prevent food and drinks slopping into passengers' laps.

At the South American refuelling ports, fresh coal supplies were poured into the ship's bunkers, coating every surface with a black layer of dust, including clothing, hands and faces. Passengers had to go below at such times so crewmen could wash the vessel down.

If Alice travelled in saloon class, she would at least have eaten well. A surviving *Aorangi* menu features dishes like spring macaroni soup, mutton cutlets à la princess, and roast turkey with sausages. If you fancied dessert, there were pastries, steamed pudding, orange jelly, and sponge cakes. All a far cry from the thin porridge and grey stew then being served up daily to Scott in his cell.

Possibly she often retreated to a room called the Ladies Boudoir. It gave women a place to meet when braying menfolk and their tobacco smoke were dominating the saloon.

---

* Shipboard life on the *Aorangi,* Edith Goodman diary, National Library of New Zealand, Alexander Turnbull Library, Ref number MSX-7042

Monday morning, 27 March, was the start of the trial's second week. The *Herald* noted the previously ailing Mr Green was in his 'usual health and spirits'. At 10am, Edwin Hesketh launched into his case for the defence. He wanted to finish it that day.

I wonder how Scott felt as he climbed the steps to the dock to face the restless, eager onlookers – 'a very large attendance of spectators', said one report. There was so much circumstantial evidence against him. He was, after all, the only one with William Thompson on the night he died, the only one sharing William's house in the weeks before then and the only one preparing his food. He'd failed to take William to a doctor. And he'd been suspiciously close to Alice – he'd even told Mrs Groves she was his 'girl'.

The jury heard that only days after she'd given birth he was visiting her bedroom. That was scandalous then – a man who wasn't Alice's husband seeing her about twice a week when the infant was merely days old!

Did Scott study Eric in his cradle, wondering if he was his own son? Did he and Alice talk about that? William, apparently fit and healthy, called in to see his wife only once when little Eric was five days old. The undelivered letter he wrote to his mother made it clear he saw Eric as *his* baby boy, but of course it would have been unthinkable to voice any doubts about parentage to his family.

Then there were the letters, especially the damning one signed 'Bertie'.

There was the analyst's opinion as to the strychnine he'd found.

There was all of Scott's shopping for poisons under false names, the pawning of Alice's jewellery and his possession of her chemises.

There was the birth-control pessary, which she had blurted was hers but which, amazingly, she'd given to Scott to keep for her. The box contained instructions for use, reported the *Herald*, with 'a printed diagram of the female organ'. All of it was handed around the jurors for inspection. It must have been a challenge for men of a more prudish mind.

How could the defence team convince them that there was enough doubt to allow Scott to walk free? Trying to bolster the suicide theory, Edwin Hesketh focused on Thompson's personal woes. 'He was worried and harassed about money matters and consequently despondent. The outlook for Mr Thompson was then as dark as it could be.'

Hesketh then had a new trio of medical men to call – doctors Girdler, Knight and McKellar – expecting them to say Thompson's sickness was more about 'gastric irritation' than poisoning. Strangely, a veterinarian was also on the list – the jury would soon understand why, Hesketh said.

Dr Girdler put Thompson's September illness down to bad meat. Had it been arsenic, he would have expected to hear about a different range of symptoms. The judge put a stop to the arsenic talk, saying the prosecution was alleging poisoning by strychnine.

Dr Knight also leaned towards the bad-food scenario but still favoured strychnine. When Hesketh asked Dr McKellar about arsenic, the judge again stepped in. He did not want it mentioned again as a possible cause of death. 'We do not intend, Your Honour, to suggest that,' one of the prosecution lawyers butted in.

'Of course not,' said Conolly. 'It would be absurd if you did.'

CHAPTER NINETEEN

Edwin Hesketh was then down to his last three witnesses: lawyer John Beale, William Thompson's neighbour William Carter, and his friend Captain John Herrold, who had gone to Sunnydale to offer help to Alice after Thompson died.

In 1889, Beale had drawn up a mortgage for £180 against William's Waikomiti property. Since William's death, the mortgage had been paid off. No one asked where the money had come from. Beale also said Thompson had called on him about two months before he died, wanting to borrow enough to pay off the mortgage plus an extra £80. 'I gave him no encouragement. He looked somewhat excited at the time.'

Excited, how? As in anxious, on edge or upset? 'Excited' does not seem to fit with the defence's attempts to paint Thompson as depressed. Hesketh did not ask Beale to explain. Neither did the Crown's lawyers.

Hesketh wanted his next two witnesses to speak on the deceased's state of mind. William Carter said he knew Thompson 'very well' – they'd both grown up in Burton-on-Trent. When Thompson had money he was jolly, 'and when he had not got it he was not quite so happy'.

Carter was the leader of the local brass band. Thompson was a member until about eight months before his death, when he said he couldn't attend anymore. The band missed him, so Carter asked him to rejoin.

'He said he had too much trouble on his mind. I told him he should not meet trouble halfway. He said he did not, but that it came right home to him.' When Carter urged Thompson to cheer up, he said he had enough worries to drive some men mad. 'Other people then came up, and the conversation stopped.'

Prosecutor Cooper stepped up to cross-examine. 'Did he tell you what his trouble was?'

'He hinted at it, but whether it was his wife's sickness or wickedness, I cannot say. It was one of them. Then really he could not be bothered to continue going to the band. That was it.'

Lastly came Captain Herrold, who had also known William 'very well'. The court heard for the first time that William had not just one house but two. There was another in Ellerslie, over which Herrold had a mortgage of £600. William had paid the interest regularly up until the previous May but couldn't make the payment that month and asked Herrold if he would wait for it. Herrold consented 'with pleasure', reported the *Herald*.

The interest was paid in July, three months before William's death, and the property had recently been sold by the registrar. Herrold had got his money back.

Justice Conolly didn't care. 'I don't see what happened six months after Thompson's death has to do with what happened at the time.'

However, Hesketh wasn't finished with Herrold. 'Did you speak to the deceased as to his financial position?'

Yes, said Herrold. Twice. In May, Thompson said he was hard up because his usual funds from England hadn't arrived.

Herrold went to see him in August and found him still worried about money. 'He even suggested that they [the Thompsons] had to go on "short commons" occasionally,' meaning they could afford only very meagre meals.

Hesketh probably wanted this story aired to suggest Thompson was miserable enough to contemplate suicide, but prosecutor Theo Cooper quickly quashed that idea by pointing out that his patience must have eased William's worries. 'You were in no sense proposing to press him?'

'Certainly not,' said Herrold.

'And he knew it?'

Yes indeed, Herrold confirmed.

The judge pitched in then. Did Thompson seem depressed about being short of funds?

Herrold didn't think so – 'but he did not appear in his usual natural good health and spirits'.

'Was he usually a cheerful man?'

'Particularly so.'

The next morning, on the eighth day of the trial, Hesketh declared the case for the defence closed.

Prosecutor Tole, however, was keen for William's brother Dr Charles Thompson to take the stand. Hesketh objected, wanting the jury to keep thinking William and Alice were so poor they'd not had enough to eat. But Tole stood firm. 'The Crown certainly has the right to call evidence to rebut that called by the defence,' he insisted.

'Of course you have,' said the judge. So, up stepped Charles. The dead man's brother! They'd have been wide-eyed in the ladies' gallery. How touching, how *impressive* that he'd come all the way from England to do his best for his family. Charles testified he'd never known his older brother to be anything but cheerful.

Tole wanted details of how much money William had brought out to New Zealand. Between £1000 and £2000, said Charles, adding that William also had £2000 in the brewery at home from which he derived income of £100 a year. Since leaving Burton-on-Trent he had not touched the £2000 principal.

William had also received sums of money from time to time. 'I know that £50 was sent out to pay the doctor's bills when his child died.' Charles then offered the small bombshell that two years after Alaric's death, those bills had still not been paid.

Maybe William was too proud to ask the family for financial help. He might not have wanted them to know he was struggling. Or maybe he relied so much on the interest that he didn't want the lump sum to shrink to something smaller. He was hardly broke, but those missing regular payments undermined him.

Had the £100 been sent regularly, asked Tole? There was a temporary problem, said Charles, but lately funds had been sent quarterly to Mr Thompson of Waikomiti.

Tole asked if he knew some money had accidentally gone to the far-distant South Island town of Waikouaiti. No, said Charles, possibly sighing internally at post-office carelessness. He added, finally, that William did have a Bank of New Zealand account in Auckland, though the judge did not allow any discussion as to how much it held at the time of his death.

And then it was all over. Just four steps remained – for the two legal teams to deliver closing speeches, for the judge to wrap it all up and for the jury to decide on their verdict.

CHAPTER TWENTY

In his closing speech for the defence, Edwin Hesketh did his best to deter the jury from assuming murder. After all, didn't poor William have enough domestic worries to make it understandable he might have secretly wished to end it all?

'Gone were the affections of a wife he loved. Gone were all those surroundings which were congenial to a man of his education and culture. Was it wonderful that he should feel that he had enough to drive any man mad, and to despair of life?'

Today we say 'wonderful' in a praising kind of way. Back then they used it more literally. Hesketh was asking 'was it any wonder' if Thompson was feeling desperate.

Then there was the lack of medical attention. While Scott had failed to deliver it, the lawyer also aimed a dart at Carter, William's neighbour. 'Could *he* not have found some means of getting a doctor?'

Hesketh scorned the idea that Scott put the crystal phial on the bedside chair while Roberton's back was turned. 'If Scott desired to suggest suicide he had numerous other means of strengthening such a suggestion.' And, why, asked the lawyer, had the jam dish and spoon not been analysed? 'It would be very significant if the jam had been found to contain strychnine.'

He came up with a benign reason for the odd smoothness of William's bedding. 'Who would not lift the disarranged bedclothes of a sick man and cover him up once more?' This would be natural, he insisted, for anyone who had a spark of humanity in him.

As for the letters Scott had written to Alice during her stay in Thames the previous winter, Hesketh declared they showed 'no undue familiarity'. And the 'Bertie' letter? Hesketh claimed the letter was 'quite innocent', and there was no proof the trousers that contained it belonged to Scott. Even if Scott had written it, no one knew if it had ever been sent to Alice or anyone else, or that it had ever left his possession. Hesketh pointed out that Scott had once told Carter he might already be married to another woman.

He couldn't resist raising Alice's absence from legal proceedings. Why, Hesketh asked, wasn't she called at the initial inquest? After all, she was there that day. Without hearing from her, could the jury have any faith in the prosecution? 'She must have been able to throw light upon Thompson's life, if not upon his death.'

Hesketh could not, of course, pretend there'd been nothing going on between Scott and Alice. But if Scott was already having the 'freest intercourse' with her – as the prosecution had asserted – what would be the point of killing Thompson? And if she could abandon her husband, might she not also later leave Scott? Knowing that, 'Would Scott have been tempted to murder her husband to make her his own wife?' asked Hesketh.

Hesketh pushed the suicide theory hard, heaping heavy blame on Alice. 'This was the greatest shock of all – the unfaithfulness of the wife to whom he was so devoted.'

The crystal phial cropped up again, too, with Hesketh saying Parker hadn't seen it by William's deathbed because he didn't lift the jam dish.

The judge lost patience. 'Parker swore that he did. You are putting to the jury what did not happen.'

Hesketh retorted that when Parker's group surveyed the death scene, they also did not see the basin, food and a soup plate noticed by the doctor.

The case was all circumstantial, he insisted. Even if strychnine had killed Thompson, no one knew how it had happened. Before finding Scott guilty, the jury would have to be 'convinced beyond a shadow of doubt' that he'd administered the poison.

It was now 4.30 on that late-summer day in the hot and airless courtroom. Hesketh had been talking all afternoon. He must have felt drained as he sat down.

Court was adjourned. Scott left the dock again, well aware that his fate was drawing closer. All that was left now was for Cooper to have his say and for the judge to sum up. Then, the verdict would loom.

WHEN COOPER STOOD up to speak the next morning, the room was packed and the mood expectant. Strychnine had been 'practically proved' as the cause of death, he insisted. And he declared the suicide theory was of 'the flimsiest character'. He scoffed at

Thompson's cash woes. With funds back in England and rent-earning property in Ellerslie, could 'commonsense men come to the conclusion that he was so depressed by financial worries as to take his own life?' Also, he pointed out, Thompson's mortgagee and friend, Captain Herrold, was not pushing him for payment.

Consider, said Cooper, all the stories they'd heard of William's habitual good cheer. Any depression was surely due to his bouts of sickness. It was also unlikely, said Cooper, that with a new boy just born he would still be in despair over his first son Alaric's death.

Then: Alice's infidelity. Thompson had 'not lost one atom of his confidence in his wife', Cooper claimed. 'There was no sign of domestic infelicity.'

He conceded they slept in different bedrooms, and a witness had heard Thompson mention Alice's 'sickness' or 'wickedness'. But Alice was 'just passing through one of the most critical periods of womanhood', said Cooper. It seemed clear to him that she was suffering from sickness, not wickedness.

Alice's pregnancy was never directly referred to, but then the word 'pregnant' hasn't always been seen as polite. In my own 1950s childhood I heard grown-ups talking of how women were 'in the family way', 'expecting', 'had a bun in the oven' or were 'up the duff'. Victorian euphemisms were even more vague. An 1870s letter written by one of my great-grandfathers said his wife (then expecting their second child) was approaching her 'trouble'. In the early 1800s, slang terms for pregnant even included the word 'poisoned'.

So, Alice's 'sickness' may have been about nausea. Even if the jurors had seen it in their own homes, the idea of wifely vomiting wasn't raised in court. Instead, Cooper waffled about her 'critical period of womanhood' as the reason why William would not have doubted her constancy.

Then he used Scott's letters to shred Alice's reputation. They showed, he said, that 'the most gross and improper intimacy existed'.

Hesketh had asked the jury to pay little heed to the foot-nestling tale. Cooper disagreed. A woman's 'fall', he said, was a 'gradual slipping away from virtue'. He was outraged by Scott's visits to Alice after Eric's birth. 'Going day after day into her bedroom showed continued intimacy of the most improper and objectionable kind.'

Helen Saul got a tongue lashing too. Cooper said he 'could not excuse' the nurse's conduct. It seems he expected her to shut the door in Scott's face. Cooper also took a swipe at Hesketh's suggestion that Scott might already have a wife. There was no proof of that story.

The shocking Bertie letter 'showed both motive and murderous desire', Cooper claimed. Damning points included the references to Dolly, which neighbour Mrs Groves had said was Scott's pet name for Alice. The letter was written to a woman who was the property of another man, said Cooper, and was 'key to the whole position'. It referred to someone called 'T' – who was 'undoubtedly' Thompson.

Cooper repeated the note's most damning lines: *What opportunities I am getting. I can do it at any time. I wish to God I could call you my very own.* 'Who but Scott could have done the deed?' he asked. 'What would not a man do when he was hopelessly infatuated with a certain woman?'

The lawyer then suggested Alice may have held the Bertie letter in her hands. He suggested that when Alice handed Scott the pessary for safekeeping, she could also have handed him the letter. Why didn't Scott destroy it? Criminals often overlook things, said Cooper. 'There seems at times to be a sort of fascination to prevent them from destroying all evidences of their guilt. Perhaps he might have intended to destroy it, or perhaps he did not think his room would be searched.'

Justice Conolly finally interrupted. 'There is no evidence that the letter ever reached Mrs Thompson, and I will have to direct the jury to that effect.' But how hard it must be for any jury to disregard words they've heard. Today we complain how we can't 'unsee' an unpleasant social media post. Back in 1893, the jury would also have struggled to un-hear Cooper's murder talk.

Cooper went on about Scott's use of false names when buying poisons and also reminded them of Alice's odd failure to return to Sunnydale on the day she'd planned. Something that passed between her and Scott made her change her plans. 'Might this not have been because Scott had finally nerved himself for the fatal deed, and did not wish her presence until it was over?'

So many questions. So many unknowable answers.

Cooper also asserted he had not needed to call Alice as it would not have been 'becoming'.

Lucky Alice. Today she would be suspected of being an accessory. Encouraging or planning a crime can result in prison time. But the police apparently didn't want to go there. Remember how a newspaper had called her 'cultured'? Maybe to the colonists' minds she seemed too cultured to be subjected to tough questioning.

At last Cooper took his seat. Hesketh had spoken for five hours, Cooper for three. There was only the judge's summing up to go and he was eager to put an end to the trial. They were adjourning for lunch, but he was keen to bore on during the afternoon. The Easter weekend lay ahead. Tomorrow was Wednesday. The Good Friday public holiday was looming. There were just two days to go.

CHAPTER TWENTY-ONE

Justice Conolly began his summing up by telling the jury that three points needed answering: Was strychnine the cause, was it suicide, or, if it was murder, did Scott do it?

The evidence, he grumbled, was so long that 'at least half of it might have been left out'. He vented at Dr Roberton for the terrible handwriting that had made his post-mortem report hard to read. However, Roberton had found no natural cause of death and was convinced William had been poisoned with strychnine. It was undoubtedly the cause of death, said the judge.

Then there was the question of suicide. William and Alice Thompson had been living apart and he fell ill after she left their home. A wife like this might be looked upon as an 'uncomfortable associate', he said with disdain, but pointed out that William didn't seem to complain.

While the dead man may have been sometimes short of cash, 'he was not actually pressed for money', said the judge. Only Scott had suggested suicide and his tales of William being despondent were 'absolutely untrue'. Conolly marvelled at how many 'useless and aimless lies' Scott had told. 'It is simply extraordinary.'

Conolly also agreed with the prosecution that little Alaric's death was unlikely to have made William want to end his own life. He had a new boy, after all. Added the judge, 'Surely, to say that he was a loving and devoted father was sufficient to prove that love of his children would prevent him from deserting them.'

What was more, the last person other than Scott to see him alive – 'the girl Kennerley' – found him 'quite cheerful'.

Then up came the phial again. The judge was not convinced the dutiful neighbours had accurately noted everything in the dead man's room. Perhaps, he said, they had overlooked it, despite its gleaming silver cap.

'If the prisoner placed it there while the doctor was examining the body, it would certainly be most suspicious.' But Conolly thought it more likely Scott had left it by the bed after having used it. Its ownership was a mystery and the judge couldn't resist another jab at Alice, saying whatever she knew she had 'wisely chosen to keep out of the way'.

Then the strychnine. Why, Conolly asked, had Scott bought six grains of it when he had told one of the chemists that the Rough on Rats he'd purchased earlier had already done away with troublesome stray cats?

The judge also pondered on the cause of Thompson's earlier vomiting bouts in September – arsenic or bad food. There was no evidence that Thompson had any 'unwholesome meat' in the house. On the other hand, Scott had bought arsenic. The jury may have groaned silently – *what, the arsenic question again?* William's earlier sickness might have been due to arsenic, said Conolly, but not if it was taken close to his death, 'for then it ought to have been found in the body'. And, of course, it was not.

It was now nearly six o'clock. Time to call a halt. Conolly had talked for four hours and needed, he said, 'several hours more'.

Up they all rose, minds stuffed with confusing detail, their bodies stiff from hours of sitting. Scott would have trudged down from the dock. Within twenty-four hours, he would learn his fate.

THE TRIAL'S last day was Thursday, 30 March, 1893. Aucklanders were now avid for the verdict.

Conolly quickly dealt with Alice Thompson's absence. 'Very little regard would have been given to her evidence, even if she had been examined. No reliance could be placed upon anything such a woman might have said.'

The jury was then asked to consider whether Scott was a man of veracity or a habitual liar. He had, after all, used 'no less than six different names' when buying poisons.

Conolly lingered on the puzzle of the day before Thompson's death when Scott had persuaded Alice to stay away. 'That circumstance has not been explained in any way.'

There was also the question of motive. Did Scott want Thompson gone so Alice could be his? 'It was proved beyond all manner of reasonable doubt that the intimacy between the two was of a highly immoral character,' said the judge. He hammered Alice again: 'In fact, the woman had lost all sense of decency. From the first, she appeared to be a woman without much modesty, having allowed Scott in her bedroom after having known him about a month.'

When Alice was away at Thames, said Conolly, it seemed that she and Scott were writing to each other twice a week. It was 'extraordinary' that the pair should write to each other so often.

Conolly also saw Scott's pawning of Alice's jewellery as a sign of 'great familiarity'. His outrage intensified as he talked of Scott's many visits to Alice before and after baby Eric's birth. He could place 'only one construction' on his visits to her bedroom.

Then they had 'the *disgusting* fact' that the prisoner was holding Alice's preventative pessary. That she asked him to look after it proved she was 'a woman without any vestige of ordinary decency'.

The infamous 'Bertie letter', said Conolly, was undoubtedly in Scott's handwriting. He ranted again about handwriting experts, for whom he had 'the greatest contempt'.

Who was the letter meant for? 'Most probably Mrs Thompson,' said the judge, but he thought she'd never seen it. He also believed the undated letter was not written during the last six weeks of Thompson's life, for it said Mrs Thompson was away and that 'T' was in town. Mr Thompson had not gone to Auckland during that time because he was ill, said the judge, so it was clear the letter was not written then.

Wait a moment, I thought. William *did* go to town then. He'd told his mother about it in the letter Alice had neglected to post. She'd had Eric on Sunday, 19 September, and William went in to see her and the baby about five days later. Let's say Friday the 24th.

'Friday' was scribbled at the top of the Bertie letter. That date was just less than six weeks before William's death on 30 October. Scott could have sat down at Sunnydale and penned the Bertie letter that very day. 'T went to town today and has not returned,' he wrote. 'I am here waiting for him.'

Thompson's September vomiting bouts began on the 26th, soon after this final trip to town. Might Scott have had a hand in that? No one knows. On the 27th, Scott moved into William's house, ostensibly to take care of him, and stayed there until he died.

Still, the Bertie letter's timing isn't as important as its existence. It is drenched with yearning. Its final words – 'My Dolly, I won't wait much longer, I can't stand it' – reflect a man desperately in love.

Conolly's only guidance was that if jury members were satisfied the letter was written by Scott to Mrs Thompson, it was for them to say what it meant in terms of the prisoner's state of mind.

He then told Scott's defence team there were three questions they had not answered: why Scott had bought strychnine on 5 October; why he hadn't brought Alice home as planned on 29 October, the day before William died; and thirdly, there was the Bertie letter – 'not dealt with by the defence in any way whatever'.

However, he had to act, the judge said, with the utmost impartiality, especially as 'a man's life was at stake'. He asked if the defence had any other matters they wanted him to cover. I can see Conolly peering down over his spectacles as he said, 'Have I omitted anything?'

'No, thank you, Your Honour,' said Samuel Hesketh.

Conolly's final task was to remind the jury of their huge responsibility. Their verdict should be given conscientiously – 'but more especially in a case of this kind. If the man is guilty of such a terrible crime he should not escape; the man against whom such a terrible crime is proved should not go free.'

CHAPTER TWENTY-TWO

As the jury filed off to a side room at 12.35pm, Scott was taken down to the cells to await his fate. He had listened to the judge, said the *Star*, 'with stoical calmness'.

A mere twenty-five minutes later, Conolly sent for the jury and people rushed back into the court. A verdict already? Not so. Conolly merely wanted to say lunch was being delivered to the jury room. He added he would not take their verdict before two o'clock. Lunch was probably on his mind, too.

A buzz of chatter went up as the crowd dispersed again. Said the *Herald*, 'During this interval the interest of the public was very great.'

By two o'clock, the courtroom and surrounding corridors were packed, said the *Star*, with some two hundred women crowding the ladies' gallery that overlooked the main body of the court. Many were just girls, brought along by eager mothers for the best entertainment in town.

The *Star* reporter heard many guesses about which way the jurors would lean. *They will disagree. They'll hang him, certain. The jury will acquit him.* Some onlookers were even placing bets. 'Numbers of wagers were flippantly made.'

The wait was short. At ten minutes after two, the jury filed back in. The judge took his seat. Scott was brought up for the final time.

'Amidst deathlike silence,' wrote the *Star*, 'the registrar asked the jury if they had unanimously found their verdict. The reply was affirmative.'

Guilty.

The *Herald* noted Scott was 'considering the circumstances, wonderfully cool and collected, and showed hardly a sign of discomposure. He looked somewhat nervous, and pulled his moustache as though to keep down his excitement.'

Scott was silent when asked if he had anything to say. Then, 'amidst silence that was painful in its intensity', Justice Conolly put on the black cap. This showed he was about to send Scott to his death. It was not an actual cap, just a square of silk on top of the judge's wig – an old British legal tradition dating back to headgear worn in Tudor times.

Scott may barely have taken in the judge's first words about the terrible nature of the murder. 'It was aggravated by the fact that the probable inducement, if such it can be called, for this murder was your immoral relationship with the wife of the murdered man. It was also aggravated by the fact that you pretended to be his friend, and appeared to be nursing him at the time you were insidiously taking away his life.

POISONING ON PARKER ROAD 145

A New Zealand Observer sketch of the day Scott was sentenced to hang – the crowded ladies' gallery agog to hear the verdict and the crowd waiting outside to watch him being driven away. Illustration: PapersPast.co.nz

'There is but one punishment for such an offence and I must tell you that you can hope for no mercy in this world.' Scott heard he was to be 'hanged by the neck until you are dead'. And finally, the last solemn line: 'May God have mercy on your soul.'

The judge's voice became so husky as he finished that he could hardly be heard. 'The prisoner received the sentence in silence and calmly, standing with his head slightly bent and his hands resting on the rail in the front of the dock,' reported the *Star*. 'The final scene showed him to be a man possessed of enormous power of control over his nerves.'

As soon as the judge was done, a warder in the dock touched Scott on the shoulder and he turned to leave. There was a huge flurry as 'the women in the gallery craned their necks over in their efforts to catch a last glimpse of him, and the crowd below pressed forward to see his face and to watch him as he passed down'.

A horse-drawn van was waiting behind the court and 'another rush of excited women' pushed close to try to catch a glimpse of him climbing on board.

The *New Zealand Observer*, a popular weekly Auckland paper, employed a clever artist whose pen-and-ink sketches capture moments from that day. They show Scott in a crisp shirt and smartly cut jacket, with groomed sideburns and a thick moustache, standing in the dock as he received his sentence.

We can see the gallery full of women gawping down over the railing. They are wearing chic little hats and dresses with leg o-mutton sleeves. Outside, a helmeted policeman struggles to hold back the excited crowd as Scott climbs into the back of the Black Maria (slang for prison van). There's also a sketch, presumably drawn from the artist's imagination, of Scott in prison garb marked with black arrows as he later receives spiritual advice from a massively bearded William Cowie, the Anglican Bishop of Auckland.

The arrows were the convicts' mark, stamped on every prisoner's rough jacket and trousers back then. Scott would not wear his own clothes again until the morning he dressed for his hanging.

CHAPTER TWENTY-THREE

The *Auckland Star* said it was 'one of the most celebrated trials in the annals of the criminal history of this colony'. But looking back from the present, so much is missing, such as any understanding of Scott's mental state. His uncle spoke of Scott's boyhood 'brain fever', his strange habit of collecting things and the trouble he'd been in over fraud. And yet many people spoke of how he seemed perfectly normal and sound of mind.

Outside of the passionate Bertie letter, his notes to Alice are lucid and well phrased. They're alive with affection. Possibly his mention of 'kisses to baby' may really have symbolised kisses meant for Alice rather than little Alfgar.

In the twenty-first century Scott would undergo a full psychiatric assessment to judge his fitness to stand trial, but back then it was sound morals, not soundness of mind, that mattered most. The judge spoke in withering tones of 'impropriety' and 'wickedness' and used words like 'disgusting' and 'highly immoral' to describe the lovers' relationship. Conolly had not even wanted Alice in his courtroom, 'considering the sort of person she was'.

Aside from all that hostility, so much else about the case was flimsy. Forensic science was in its infancy, so all the talk about tissue analysis came from only one man, Mr Pond. There was no modern scene examination. Most medical men in the witness box had not seen Thompson in life, or in death, and could only deliver assumptions. There were many opinions and few facts. No one could even say for sure when he had taken his last breath.

Given the judge's contempt for handwriting experts, he'd have been furious if he could have known that more than a hundred years after the trial an uppity woman (me) would commission just such a person to supply insights into the character of William Thompson.

I'd worked once before with a graphologist when I included a handwriting analysis column in a monthly magazine I edited called *Next*. It was very popular in the 1990s, with a booming circulation. Celebrities, TV stars and politicians willingly sent in samples of handwriting for our graphologist, Marie Davis, to analyse. Readers' anonymous samples were included too.

Marie saw handwriting as 'frozen body language'. She told me it could reveal people's psychology and personality traits, and was commonly used in Europe by counsellors and psychotherapists, and by employers wanting insights into the character of job applicants.

She would comment on arcane details such as margin size, loops, terminal strokes and baselines to present a picture of each person. I've lost track of her, but when I discovered Thompson's will in the files of Archives New Zealand, I was curious to see if his scrawl might offer clues as to his character.

This time I found Aucklander Mike Maran. A forensic graphologist, he is mostly hired by lawyers, private detectives, businesses and institutions looking for expert assessment of documents to verify signatures. Writing by hand may be a dying habit, but as Maran says, 'We are still largely paper based, especially in legal areas.' He is a certified member of the US-based Scientific Association of Document Examiners.

Occasionally, however, someone like me asks him to report on what a person's writing reveals about their character. 'Graphology will never get that a hundred per cent right,' he told me. 'We humans are much too complex for that, but it can certainly give you an indication of the kind of person you're looking at.'

His report on William Thompson was intriguing, as I'd said nothing about who he was. Maran presents his analysis in the present tense because he reads writing not as a historic document but as if it's been put on paper today. Some of the comments popped out at me.

Remember how William didn't really want to be a lawyer? Maran's report said: 'Because William is super-independent, he feels resentful at what he considers the heavy-handed use of authority. No confining ties that bind for him.' Of course, William had left his family and home country behind and went away as far as possible.

Remember how he and Alice had separate bedrooms? Report: 'In his sex life, William is likely to be ultraconservative and conventional. He continually checks his sexual performance, afraid it will not live up to his partner's expectations and desires.'

So, was this why Alice was drawn to Alexander Scott? Perhaps he excited and delighted her in a way her husband couldn't.

Remember William's rejection of his friend Carter's suggestion that Scott might be poisoning him? Report: 'He will not part with information. Even relatively minor details are kept secret. He baulks when it comes to dealing with a conflict or problem directly and sidesteps the issue in an attempt to divert the other person's attention to something less stressful.' The outcome: William's resistance to dealing with that disturbing question meant Carter decided not to mention it again.

Remember how Scott called Sunnydale the House of Desolation? Report on William: 'He seems to look for the downside in every situation. No matter how well things are going, he will find a flaw somewhere.' The outcome: Alice probably felt demoralised by William's down moods and found in Scott someone who sympathised with her unhappiness and made her feel better.

Remember all the comments about how cheerful Thompson was? Report: 'It seems he is afraid he will be rejected if he opens himself up and shows what is in his heart. Even though he may feel awkward and isolated, he can't bring himself to demonstrate his feelings.'

Rumours. Snippets. Comments. Secrets. Much more than a century later, it's impossible to know exactly what was going on in all their hearts. Which just leaves fact. William Thompson died along with his dreams of a better life. Scott was found guilty of his murder. He, too, would soon be gone.

CHAPTER TWENTY-FOUR

The authorities took great care in preparing for Scott's execution. They even did some landscaping, spreading fresh gravel on the path to the scaffold. Shortly before 8am on the drizzly morning of 22 May 1893, the jail bell tolled twice to signal his end was near. Observers wrote of the *crunch, crunch* sound made by boots on that gravel as Scott and the official party approached.

The jailer, Mr Reston, led the medical officer, Dr Philson, followed by two warders and then Alex Scott, bare-headed and walking a little stiffly because his arms were tightly bound to his sides. The chaplain, Rev William Calder, came last in his white surplice.

'There were altogether about eighteen witnesses,' wrote the *New Zealand Herald*'s reporter, 'but from the first tones of the chaplain's voice, not another sound was heard, save the steady tread of the processionists as they crossed the courtyard. All was hushed and still, the spectators scarcely allowing themselves to breathe.'

Calder had officiated at William Thompson's funeral nearly six months earlier. He had become Scott's main spiritual adviser during his time in jail and would also preside at his burial.

The Crown already had a scaffold in storage, left over from the executions of John Caffrey and Henry Penn, who had murdered a man on Great Barrier Island during a botched attempt to abduct Caffrey's daughter. They had been hanged six years earlier.

As Scott waited, he might have heard the hammering as workmen rigged it up again in a courtyard at the back of the jail, within a tall wooden fence. They hung canvas tarpaulins to prevent any casual onlookers from viewing the scene, either from outside the walls or from the top of the rock face that reared up behind the prison.

The last public hanging in New Zealand, in Wellington, had been thirty-five years earlier. Now, not many people loitered outside the jail, though a few hundred had climbed the hill the day before to get a glimpse of what the *Herald* called 'the engine of death'.

Calder stayed with Scott until midnight and came back at 6.30am to pray with him. Scott had been up since six. He was 'calm and collected, and did not evince any dread of approaching death', wrote the *Star*'s reporter.

How did he know that? Perhaps it was an impression later gleaned from Calder or other prison officers, who had apparently grown quite fond of the condemned man. There was a kind of respect from reporters too: 'Scott bore the horrible ordeal with an undaunted spirit,' wrote an *Auckland Star* scribe when it was all over. 'To the last he proved himself to be a man of enormous power of control over his nerves, and of a courage worthy of a better end.'

Scott had written farewell messages to relatives. Added the *Star* with a tone of regret, 'Of course, they are strictly confidential.'

Calder left Scott alone then so he could swap his convict gear for his own clothes – moleskin trousers and a clean white shirt, with a handkerchief wrapped around his waist. He had some breakfast – a little tea and toast – and 'indulged in a smoke'.

The chaplain returned at 7.30 for more prayers and readings. Scott asked him to read Hymn 289 in the *Ancient and Modern Hymnal*, which begins, 'Days and moments quickly flying, blend the living with the dead. Soon will you and I be lying, each within his narrow bed …'

When Calder had finished, he told Scott that by 'a curious coincidence', the very same hymn had been chosen earlier by his own congregation at All Saints Church in Ponsonby, and was at that moment being sung by them. Calder had earlier asked his parishioners to attend a brief intercessory service to coincide with when Scott was scheduled to die. More than two hundred crowded the church that morning to pray for him.

This, according to the *Herald*, was to strengthen 'him and his friend' as the ordeal approached. His friend? Maybe the two men did become somewhat close as they talked in the weeks before the execution. One of their conversations probably disturbed Calder, as Scott revealed he had previously shot 'an Aboriginal man' while working in Queensland. He offered the story as a kind of proof of innocence. The face of the man still haunted him, he said, while he had no such feelings when he recalled the face of William Thompson.

There had been no trouble over the first death, as the man was wanted for some minor crime. In Australia then, a dead Aborigine would have been of little concern to Queensland authorities. I searched *Trove*, Australia's online newspaper archives, and could find no mention of a shooting involving Scott.

Scott assured Calder that he would not break down 'and there would be nothing approaching a scene on his part'. Apparently, staying staunch was expected. Scott was silent as he was formally told that the government would not stop the carrying out of his sentence. He shook hands with his jailers and warders and thanked them for their kindness.

The executioner stepped forward with a leather strap to bind Scott's arms, crossed in front of him, before they set off on his final walk. 'Have mercy upon me, oh God, after thy great goodness,' Calder was heard to intone as they approached the scaffold.

The *Herald* reported Scott had grown a beard since last seen in public, and he came forward with a 'firm, quick, and buoyant step'. He looked pale, and somewhat thinner than at the trial. 'With a swift and piercing glance at each spectator, he swept the courtyard with his restless eyes, which seemed to have a sort of hunted expression, but he never faltered.'

Still Calder droned on: 'Make me a clean heart, oh God, and renew a right spirit within me.' Scott then climbed the eleven steps to the top. The bell was slowly tolling all this time. 'Without a pause he mounted up, and with no sign of hesitation he planted his feet upon the fatal trapdoors.' There were two doors hinged at the sides, so as they fell away he would drop through the central gap.

Alert for any sign of weakness, the *Herald*'s man wrote: 'Perhaps it was the slight give of the trapdoors, but as he stood there a quiver seemed to pass over his frame; otherwise his nerve did not for a moment fail him.'

The hangman, black-hatted and elderly with grey side-whiskers, stepped behind him to pinion the legs. Now came Scott's chance to say his last words. Calder had helped him write a statement. The *Star* said he spoke it 'brokenly and in a husky voice': 'I stand here to make the confession that I have sinned grievously against God. This I have said to the chaplain and I have made my peace with God. My conscience is broken down and I can do no more.'

But then his voice rose as if he was keen speak his own mind. 'I am innocent,' he declared. 'I have taken this upon myself to save another and I have carried it through.' He again thanked the jailer and other officers 'for their kind consideration' and said his lawyers had been friends as well as solicitors.

At this point came 'a few seconds of painful silence and suspense'. Calder pressed him again, asking if he had anything else to add. 'I am perfectly innocent in this matter,' Scott repeated. 'I have taken it upon myself to save another.' He muttered, according to another report, about a promise made and kept.

And that was it.

THE *HERALD* THOUGHT he had meant to give 'a more connected and longer speech, but failed to do so for lack of words'. Reston had previously advised him not to try to say too much: 'Men about to die generally broke down if they spoke for too long, as the excitement became too great.'

Another long prayer came from Calder's mouth, full of sentiments about mercy, pity and the hope that God would give Scott repentance for his 'wilful and gross sin'.

Scott began to tremble as the executioner, who 'went about his gruesome duties with perfect coolness', drew a white hood over his head, followed by the noose, which was tightened to set the 'thimble' (the knotted part) under Scott's ear. Then the hangman went to the other side of the platform, pulled the bolt, the trap fell open and Scott fell.

'The sound of a falling body brought up with a sudden jerk was heard,' the *Herald* wrote. 'Then all was still and after the first rebound the rope did not oscillate, and from the absence of any vibration it was evident that the man had been killed instantaneously.'

Officials had planned things with a terrible kind of efficiency. Though the floor of the scaffold was more than three metres high, a deep hole was dug beneath it to avoid any possibility of Scott's feet hitting the ground when he dropped. And they had padded the underpart of the scaffold to prevent any rebound of the trapdoor.

When it was over, the hangman scooted down a front set of stairs to make sure Scott was, as the *Star* put it, 'extinct'. His neck was broken and he was dead. The rule was that the body must hang for an hour before being cut down, and none of the official observers was allowed to leave the jail during that time. So they went inside out of the rain. What happened then? A sustaining cup of tea or a swig or two of whisky? The hardest of men must have found it an awful experience. Except perhaps for the hangman, Tom Long.*

He was not named in any of the Auckland newspapers at the time, but two years later, when he handled the Invercargill execution of Minnie Dean – the only woman ever hanged in New Zealand – he

---

* Tom Long, hangman, https://teara.govt.nz/en/photograph/26489/tom-long-hangman & https://paperspast.natlib.govt.nz/newspapers/NZTR19200626.2.36

took a local reporter on a preview tour of the scaffold to explain how well he would do his job.

The rope he would use, said Long, was the same one he'd employed for the hanging of Alexander Scott. He cheerily pointed out the advantages it had over the one the Invercargill authorities had provided. It became, said the reporter, 'sickening to listen to'.

Hangman Tom Long was a 19th century celebrity in New Zealand – well known for his grisly trade. Photo: Manatū Taonga Ministry for Culture & Heritage, Wairarapa Archive

Now, having just dispatched Scott, he could walk away, but the other men in attendance still had work to do. After the body was taken down it was laid on a wooden bench. Reporters didn't hold back from describing how the dead man looked, as they knew that *Herald* readers would be wanting detail. The head lolled loosely, and 'the face appeared placid, there being a bluish tint over a portion of the features, and a deep groove around the neck made by the rope'. It also noted 'the features were more calm than is usual in cases of hanging'.

Dr Philson, the prison surgeon, examined the body before declaring him officially deceased. Maybe it was he who removed a ring from Scott's finger. It was a woman's three-stoned ring, with one stone missing. Scott had asked if he could wear the ring at his death and if it could then be sent to his lawyers so they could ensure it went to 'a certain lady friend'.

Was this Alice? We will never know. By then she was back in England. Having sailed away three months earlier, she was far from the bleak scene in Auckland. Alice might have been horrified later to hear what Scott said just before he dropped, for in taking his punishment to 'save another', he heaped suspicion straight on her head. Who else could that 'other' be but her?

CHAPTER TWENTY-FIVE

It was common after an execution for reporters to be allowed to visit the dead man's cell. Scott had had two – one for daytime use and another to sleep in, plus an 'airing yard' for when he wanted some solo exercise. In trooped the curious writers. There wasn't much to see – a messily made narrow bed, a few apples on a shelf, a basin, a mug and a stack of books.

Perhaps, as a condemned man, he was allowed the luxury of some fruit. Prison meals, as outlined in Mark Derby's *Rock College: An unofficial history of Mount Eden Prison*, were monotonously dreadful: porridge and bread morning and night and boiled beef and vegetables, including rotten potatoes, at midday.[*]

His books included a Bible and other tomes of spiritual advice, such as *A Manual of Devotions*, no doubt supplied by Rev Calder. There was a copy of *All the Year Round*, a weekly journal created

---

[*] Prison food, *Rock College: An unofficial history of Mount Eden Prison*, Mark Derby, Massey University Press, 2020.

by Charles Dickens as a vehicle for his own serialised stories. The author had been dead more than twenty years by the time an issue found its way into Scott's cell.

One book was tucked under the head of his mattress to create a kind of pillow. Scott also had two novels – *Alaric Spenceley* by Mrs J H Riddell* and *An Australian Heroine* by romance writer Rosa Praed.† In writing about the 'iron nerve' Scott had displayed in court, the *Otago Witness* reported that he'd stayed calm as he awaited his execution, 'occupying his time for the most part in reading, his weakness being fiction'.

The *Witness* obviously thought it odd for a hard man from Melbourne to while away his time by reading books by women. Most men tended to prefer stories by male authors. Mrs Riddell did not risk using her own name, Charlotte, but instead soft-pedalled her femininity by using her husband's surname.

She was the prolific author of more than fifty books, but *Alaric Spenceley* had its detractors. 'Most people, we fancy, will find this book more or less dull,' wrote a London reviewer when it was launched. Possibly Scott had the book at his bedside as a tiny link to the mother of the little Alaric, whose grave he used to visit.

Praed's *An Australian Heroine* was also an unlikely read. Raised in Australia, the author lived most of her life in London and specialised in stories about women trapped in loveless marriages.

She wrote of a miserable fictional heroine, Esther, and her husband: 'Between him and Esther there always seemed a barrier

---

* Victorian novelist Charlotte Riddell, https://www.victorianresearch.org/atcl/show_author.php?aid=252
† Victorian novelist Rosa Praed, https://adb.anu.edu.au/biography/praed-rosa-caroline-8095

of unrealisable expectations, and of mutual incomprehension. Neither knew quite how to approach the other.'

Perhaps that was a factor in the Thompsons' marriage. Perhaps Scott read, or re-read, that book as his death approached, trying to convince himself that his Alice was one of many unhappy wives in the world, and that he – like all the heroes in Praed's tales – had good reason for rescuing her from the House of Desolation.

There was a brief inquest at the jail that morning, with a coroner present to hear a jury confirm that Scott had duly died. The body was released to Scott's uncle John Wilson. Optimistically, Scott had picked out some words for his gravestone – a few lines from a hymn called *Lead, Kindly Light*. But gravestones cost money and apparently no one was willing to pay: his plot remains unmarked.

He also asked that he be buried alongside William Thompson in the little Ōrātia Cemetery. That plea was ignored. The very idea was probably seen as outrageous. Instead, they put him in the Church of England part of the huge cemetery by the railway station – it being unthinkable then for the bodies of Protestants and Catholics to be laid close to each other.

Scott's coffin was taken to an unnamed friend's house in nearby Newton for the night and then loaded into a horse-drawn hearse early the next day for a wet two-hour trip out to the cemetery. There was almost no one to farewell Scott – just a friend named Griffiths from his Australian schooldays and his uncle John, no doubt utterly worn down by the nightmare of having his wayward nephew come to live with him.

Lawyers Edwin and Sam Hesketh, who'd tried so hard to keep him from the gallows, were also there. And presiding over the burial was the man with the ever-present prayer book, William Calder.

He'd wanted so badly to prevent the hanging that he sent a last-minute telegram to the government maintaining Scott was not guilty due to being 'morally insane'. The Hesketh brothers had also drawn up affidavits seeking a pardon on grounds of insanity. None of it worked.

In reporting on the execution, the *Star* said, 'It may be in place to state here that Scott's mother, father and sisters are quite convinced of his innocence.'

Over in Geelong, his family must have been embarrassed to read the coverage of their Alex's conviction and death in their local newspapers. Australian papers took a lurid approach as they described Scott's 'fiend-like atrocity', the 'illicit intercourse' and the 'disgusted neighbours' who had seen unsettling signs of the lovers' scandalous liaison.

It seems Australia was reluctant to claim him as one of their own. A story about him in the *Melbourne Herald* only mentioned in the final paragraph that he had relatives in Western Victoria, but did not say he was Geelong born and bred.

But the *Auckland Star* didn't let him off lightly either. On the day of his execution, it told its readers that 'for calm, cold-blooded, systematic treachery, Scott's crime is not surpassed by any murder recorded in the criminal annals of the colony'.

ON THE DAY that Carolyn Melling and I first met, she took me not only to William Thompson's imposing headstone in the sweet little Ōrātia graveyard but also to the rear of Glen Eden's busy shopping strip to see where Scott lies. His unmarked grave in the vast Waikumete Cemetery is close to where Auckland's western railway line runs between the shops and the cemetery's rear boundary. Electric trains glide past on rails once occupied by huffing steam engines. Looming over the scene are two gleaming high-rise apartment blocks – buildings of a scale and size unimaginable in Victorian times.

Carolyn knows the spot from its proximity to other more obvious graves, but it's not easy to find. In this old part of the cemetery, the words chiselled into mossy gravestones are worn down and illegible – the occupants so long deceased that the only visitors are dog walkers or those who like picking a posy of the pretty meadow flowers that pop up there in spring. As we stood on Scott's bare plot, a brisk breeze whipping blades of rough green grass around our shoes, there was no way to know that six feet down lay what was left of a man who had once been the talk of the town.

So, after his trial and execution – after all the drama, speculation, fear and dread – which Thompsons were left behind in Auckland? Just Charles, the young doctor, already planning his passage home. And, of course, his two very small nephews, Alfgar and Eric.

PART III
RIPPLES

CHAPTER TWENTY-SIX

Meanwhile, what went on for Alice Thompson in the years after her time in the House of Desolation? The whole story is marked by her absence – not just from her husband's house back in 1892, but in the Supreme Court too. There were no insights from friends about what was going on in her head before and after her husband's death. Did she even have any Auckland friends other than her nurse, Helen Saul?

There are no personal letters to examine for clues, no diaries full of jottings. Newspapers of the 1890s talked only of her prettiness and how she'd scandalously cried out, 'That's mine!' to a policeman who held up her most intimate possession, the device for preventing pregnancy.

She was the case's scarlet woman, scorned in court every time her name was mentioned. Everyone, from the judge down, assumed she chose to run away during Scott's trial. But how do we know she wanted to scarper? Did the Thompsons – represented by her brother-in-law Charles – say she must return by herself, without even the comfort of having her small sons travel with her?

Many Aucklanders probably suspected she encouraged Scott in his bid to do away with her husband, but there is no proof of that. She might have been oblivious to everything except her attraction to Scott.

If Alice was wildly in love with him, did that soon change to a rush of shame that she'd been taken in by his wily charms? Reading the newspaper reports about his case would have been unbearable – and even worse when things began to look worse and worse for him – and for her, too.

Presumably, after the hanging, news reached her in England about how Scott seemed to implicate her with his final words about how he had promised to shield another person.

It's easy to assume the ring he wore on the scaffold was meant for her. Was she the lady friend Scott said it should be mailed to? Only his legal team, the Hesketh brothers, would have known, as Scott had made them responsible for sending it on. After watching his coffin going into the dank earth, forwarding the ring would have been the last task they could perform for their client.

She stepped ashore in England towards the end of March 1893 – possibly on the very day Justice Conolly sentenced Scott to death. And then she'd have faced a series of excruciating conversations with her own family – and, especially, William's. Awkward and painful for everyone.

Later on, her life would be marked by frequent bouts of poor health. They seemed to happen in the first few weeks of the year. Perhaps she hated January.

In the week I wrote those words, a friend of mine mentioned it was almost the anniversary of her husband's sudden death in a mountaineering accident. 'It's more than twenty years ago,' she said, 'but there's something about this time of year that I always find hard.' Maybe Alice was often struck by the January blues.

Her toddler, Alaric, had died in January of 1891 and that month also marked the awful time, two years later, that Alice endured in Auckland when Alex Scott was about to go on trial for murder, her reputation was in shreds, and her future must have looked terribly bleak.

Two decades on, in her mid-forties, her life might not have seemed any more hopeful. No wonder, perhaps, if dwelling on those earlier crises sometimes made her take to her bed. Occasionally, census records note a female visitor being in her house, but she never seems to have partnered with another man.

WHAT WAS Alice's life like after she returned to England? Twenty years before I stumbled over this story, Thompson family historian Monica Leat had already found out some of what happened next. The family story was that Dr Charles Thompson had brought Alfgar and Eric back home. I've found no proof of that, but it must be what older family members told her. Who cared for the boys in the two months after Alice departed and before Charles boarded his ship? It's not known. Whatever happened, they did later grow up in England.

In New Zealand's archives of outbound passenger lists I found a Dr Charles Thompson, aged twenty-seven, who sailed from Lyttelton for London via Rio de Janeiro in saloon class on 24 April

1893, aboard the 6127-ton *Ruahine*, then the biggest ship on the New Zealand run.*

This must have been the right Charles, for the *Otago Witness* reported that he'd left Auckland two weeks earlier and headed south to pick up the 'direct steamer' for home, feeling 'very much distressed at the tragic close of his brother's career'. The *Ruahine* sailed a month before Scott climbed up the gallows steps. There were one hundred and seventy-eight 'souls on board', including twenty-five children and two infants.

There was no mention of Charles's nephews, Alfgar and Eric. While the family legend says Charles took them home, such stories can get fudged over the years, and the boys don't appear in the *Ruahine*'s passenger list. Names of some of the children on board were included, but not Alfgar. Not Eric. If they were travelling with their uncle, would he have hired a nursemaid for the trip? It would have been unusual for a single man to care for a little boy and a baby on such a long voyage. The Thompsons could no doubt afford a nurse. A one-way saloon-class (first-class) ticket cost 60 guineas – more than £6000 in today's money.†

When the *Ruahine* was launched in London a year earlier, a *Press* correspondent praised its 'enormous' upper deck space and the bright and cheerful saloon, with 'one of the prettiest and snuggest of fireplaces imaginable'. Cosy coal fires were quite the thing then for keeping saloon-class passengers warm in cold latitudes.

Charles would have made sure Alice tidied up William's debts,

---

* Ships' passenger lists, www.familysearch.org
† Measuring worth of old currency, https://www.measuringworth.com/calculators/ukcompare/relativevalue.php

settling all the bills to doctors, pharmacists and horse hirers that Scott had put on the Thompson account.

Only one day after William's death, solicitor Frederick Baume put a probate document in front of Alice. She duly signed it. It said her husband had appointed her the sole executrix of his will. Her signature meant that she promised to pay 'the debts and legacies of the deceased as far as the property will extend and the law binds'. The estate was valued at 'not more than £1000'. The actual amount was not given.

I found the document in online archives, along with William's will. He had scrawled it in splashy ink on 9 May 1892, nearly six months before he died. It was witnessed by his neighbour William Carter – and by Alexander Scott. Everything went to Alice.

The will wasn't mentioned during the murder trial, but months earlier Carter had told the inquest about the day on which it was written. He said Scott had called out to him that he thought he and William had been poisoned. Carter arrived to find William eating tobacco – 'I'm trying to make myself vomit,' he said. And he did so, violently. Carter said he seemed scared.

The men decided that there could have been something in the tea they'd been drinking. Alice wasn't home that day, but they thought she might have left something on a kitchen shelf that had fallen and affected the tea. They later put it down to bad meat. When asked, Carter said he'd not seen Scott vomiting, he'd witnessed only William's illness.

Maybe this sudden, vile sickness frightened William so much that he thought he should make a will that very day – or maybe he was nudged by his friends. He was a lawyer, after all, so knew how to write one. He could pick up a pen and do it right away. And when Scott signed as a witness at the foot of the page, it meant he now knew that if William Thompson should die, all of his worldly goods would go to Alice. Was the knowledge of her inheritance status another reason for his pursuit of her?

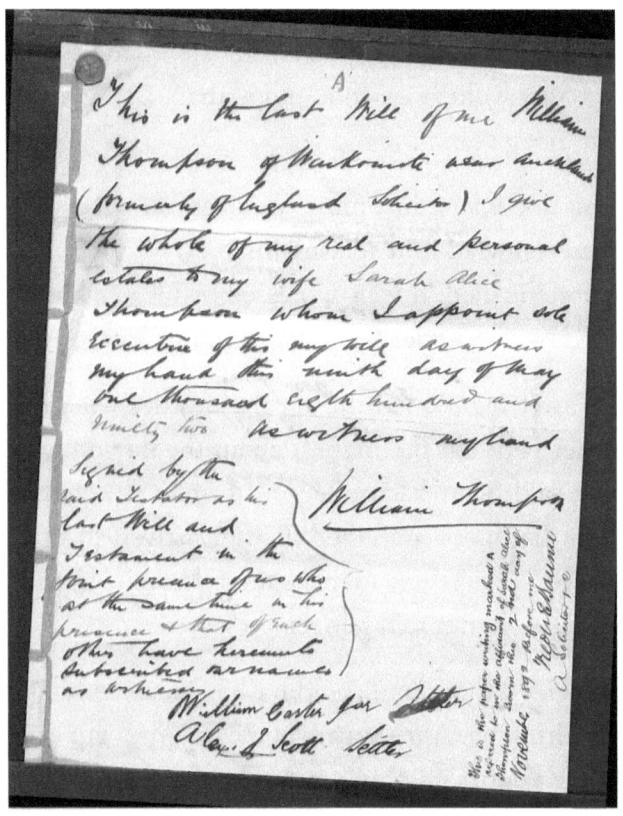

William's hurriedly scrawled will, penned on a day he'd been ill five months before his death. One of the witnesses who signed at the foot of the page was Alexander Scott, the man who would later be charged with William's murder.
Image: Archives New Zealand

Alice or Charles must have ordered the imposing headstone over William and Alaric's shared grave. I wonder if Charles ever saw it and noticed the misspelling of Alaric's name. He might have demanded it be redone. Or, more likely, he was so eager to leave the whole dreadful mess behind that he just shrugged and let it be.

Once the boys were back in England, decisions had to be made. The Thompsons would have been horrified by Alice's behaviour. However, here were William's boys, needing to be nurtured. But by whom?

The outcome was that Alfgar was raised mainly in Burton-on-Trent, largely cared for in his early years by an uncle and aunt. But the boys lived largely apart. Eric stayed with Alice, who moved around a succession of other towns, mostly on England's south coast and in Wales.

Proof of that comes from a pile of tiny diaries in which Alfgar jotted daily notes from 1906 to 1913. They were all in the box of documents I received from Nick Frost, kept in his attic for many years. Unwrapping the diaries melted my heart. It was amazing to be able to hold those little old books, still in good condition and rarely opened but still treasured.

Smaller than palm-sized, they'd have been just right for Alfgar to tuck into vest and trouser pockets. Most are leather bound, worn soft and smooth more than a century ago by his constant handling. In the years before World War I, he was as attached to his diaries as we are today to our phones. Almost every day contains an entry dashed down in tiny writing. They reveal the life of a carefree, outdoorsy young man.

He turned seventeen in 1906 and would have had only faint memories, if any, of New Zealand, which he left when he was barely four years old. Now he was living a charmed *Boy's Own* kind of life, charging round the countryside and being a danger to woodland creatures. Educated at Burton Grammar School, he must have decided mechanical engineering would be his life's work but there are no records of where he learnt those skills. His brother Eric's schooling is unknown.

In a section of the 1906 diary called Game Bag, Alfgar kept count of birds he shot: 3 January, one sparrow; 8 January, eight sparrows; 9 January, one starling – then two, three and four starlings on subsequent days. On 3 January, he also scribbled that he'd taken back a library book for Eric, took a football to be re-stitched (three pennies), bought a dozen little targets (three more pennies) and also 'smashed a pane of glass in our greenhouse'.

On the shooting went. On 14 April of that year he did away with five sparrows and a waterhen. For variation over the months there were chaffinches, green linnets, snipes, pigeons and plenty of rabbits. The killing of small game, birds and fox cubs went on and on in subsequent years. Little did he know what a useful skill he was developing. World War I would begin in just eight years. When it erupted, he joined up fast, entering the British Army aged twenty-five in 1914 and quickly being promoted to sergeant. He served in France in 1915 and must have been what the military calls 'officer material', for by 1916 he was a second lieutenant in the Machine Gun Corps.

Back in his sunny teen years, life wasn't all about shooting. His jottings skip through school, tennis, fishing, and swimming in summer and ice skating in winter. He played parlour games like whist, bagatelle and fives and took dancing lessons – 'Reversed two and half times around the room with Miss Marion', he wrote in one diary with a satisfied flourish.

Alfgar Thompson, Machine Gun Corps officer in World War I. Photo: Nick Frost collection

CHAPTER TWENTY-SEVEN

The Thompsons were Church of England people who made regular family visits to the cemetery as well as to church. Alfgar was usually in the pews every Sunday, sometimes twice (at 8am and 11am), and there was often hymn singing at home at night. 'Went to church,' he wrote in 1906, when he was sixteen, adding a dry comment on the vicar's sermon: 'Maynell held forth.'

He 'tubbed' the family pet, John Dog, and played the violin as his father had done in Auckland. Alfgar's slang term for it was 'scraping'. He fitted in work described as 'hooking' or 'booking' (his tiny writing is so hard to decipher), which was no doubt some brewery task. He also went to boxing practice and drawing class, mowed lawns, attended drill, bought books from Daileys bookshop and sometimes played 'footer' in the afternoon. An evening talk hints at an interest in where he was born. 'Went to lecture by Mr Andrews on natural history of New Zealand. Very good. Took notes.' There were lessons in 'ambulance practice', learning how to handle injuries and apply bandages.

Alfgar (seated) and Eric lived mainly apart in boyhood but were together in this studio portrait taken in Canterbury, England. The pet may be John Dog, whom Alfgar mentions in his teenage diaries. Photo: Nick Frost collection

As the years spun by there were frequent nights out at plays and musicals. Mostly, though, the diaries are a long trudge through days on which all he wrote about was his daily routine: study, work, church, football, shooting, catching trains, family dinners etc. There is no introspection – little indication of how he *felt* about anything.

Odd little echoes seemed to chime down through the years as I scanned his seven diaries. On 6 October 1909, he enjoyed a production of *The Merry Wives of Windsor*. On the day I read that note, I happened to drive past the What's On sign outside an Auckland high school. It made me smile to see it was staging the very same musical more than a century later.

In Burton-on-Trent, with no father and a distant mother, he sailed along beneath the wings of extended family – his Thompson grandparents, aunts, uncles and cousins. Cruising between three family homes in the town, he enjoyed dinner here, tennis there, an overnight stay somewhere else.

Alfgar seems to have loved his Auntie Lena (wife of Dr Charles Thompson). His frequent visits with her are often underlined, especially if she gave him a treat. 'Lena made toffee!' he wrote one day. She taught him dance steps, too, and his uncle Charlie, who had rescued Alfgar and Eric from New Zealand, was a favourite fishing, shooting and tennis companion.

The 1908 diary was the only one missing from the stack of little diaries. I was puzzled when Alfgar stopped mentioning Lena in his 1909 jottings. She'd obviously been one of his favourite people – and then, she vanished. I eventually learnt she had died in 1908, aged only forty-one. Charles and Lena were married for just ten years. They had no children. So, here was another Thompson family tragedy.

I ordered her death certificate from the very efficient British GRO – the General Registry Office. The charming Lena was eaten up by cancer of the colon, perineum and ovaries. It must have been horrifying for Charles, for he'd have known her death was inevitable and all his medical skills would have been useless except for giving her a degree of pain relief.

After that, even though Lena was gone, Alfgar still noted her birthday, 10 November, in the back of his 1910 and 1911 diaries. Coincidentally, the day of her birthday was also the day on which she died.

The brothers lived mostly separate lives. Eric's name crops up mostly around Christmas and again in summer, when Alfgar would take trains to go to stay with Alice and his brother for a month or so. She moved around over the years – his diaries mention many different towns and railway stations transited on his holiday breaks.

Alice must have pleaded for at least one of her boys to stay close to her, and Eric was the natural choice. The Thompsons were decent people and would have wanted to see him as one of their own, but doubt must have niggled away at them – was he really William's boy? Or was he the son of Scott, William's killer?

Only Alice knew with whom she'd had sex, and when. If she'd been with both men at around the same time, there was of course no way in the nineteenth century to establish the truth. Carolyn and I talked about it one day in the room that had once been William's parlour, studying formal photos taken of the brothers as boys and young men.

Handsome lads they were – especially Eric. There is a brotherly resemblance. It's hard to know what, if anything, can be made of the fact that Alfgar's cleft chin is just like the one visible in his father William's boyhood studio photo. Eric's chin was smooth.

Alfgar's diary mentions of Eric are scanty – no more than blips on the page, such as 'Eric skating' or 'Met Eric – played fives with him'. And then in 1909 comes the most mysterious Eric note. On 12 May, Alfgar reported: 'Had photos taken in dinner hour. At night took Eric to the theatre – *The Country Girl* – in London.'

The next day, 13 May, his laconic entry was: 'Work as usual. Eric departed.' His brother's name is absent from the diary for the entire rest of that year. The family legend I heard via Carolyn was that Eric had been 'sent to Canada' when he was sixteen. He was sixteen that year. So was 13 May the day he departed for good?

There's no sign of anxiety on Eric's face in a professional photo of the brothers possibly taken before they went to see *The Country Girl*. They face the camera side by side wearing smart dark suits. Their smiles are slight and calm, their hair smooth and brilliantined.

A studio photo taken one Wednesday in 1909 in Alfgar's 'dinner hour', possibly the day before Eric (seated) went away to Canada at 16. Nick Frost collection

The picture is undated, but they look to be in their mid- to late teens. It's just the sort of picture that might be arranged to mark a special moment, such as just before one of them was about to go away for a very long time.

I don't know if they ever saw each other again, for from that point on they lived very different lives.

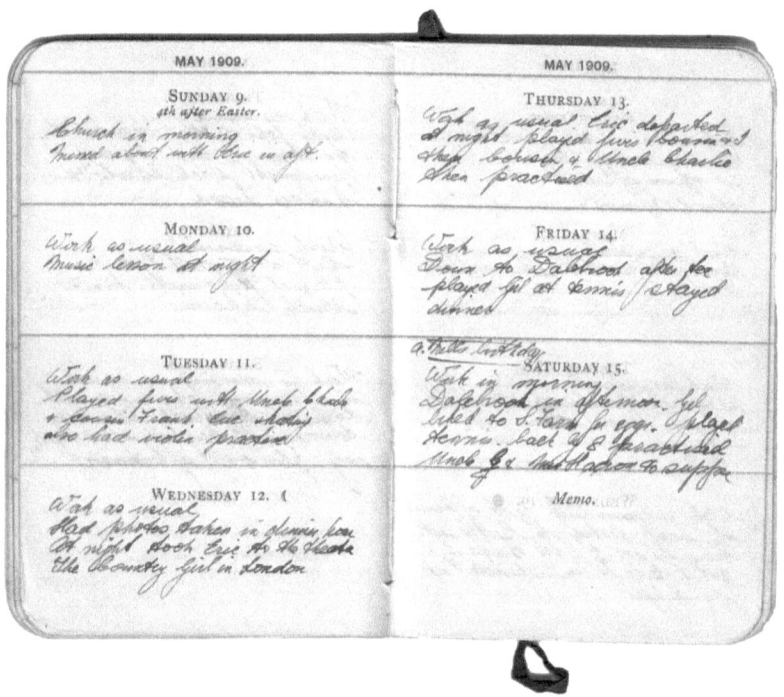

The curious note in Algar's diary on 13 May 1909 that says 'Eric departed'.
Photo: Nick Frost collection

CHAPTER TWENTY-EIGHT

Alfgar's life is easier to track, mainly because of the documents and pictures in family archives. The 1910 and 1911 diaries show Alfgar in his early twenties, working as a colliery engineer in South Wales. Coal mining was huge there then. By 1913 production was at its peak, employing two hundred and fifty thousand workers and hauling fifty-six million tons of coal out of the ground every year.

At twenty-two he's in Phillipstown, a South Wales mining village. Many of his diary entries are just 'work as usual', 'work as usual', day after day. There's plenty to do. He is dealing with hot bearings, putting in new pistons or steam pipes, getting stop valves to work or servicing the fire alarm and something called an 'economiser'.

But it's not all work. In February that year he enjoys a farewell party for a girl called Ruby, and a 'great do' where someone has a phonograph that plays music recorded on cylinders. Finally, people can enjoy hearing recorded music instead of making it themselves. After this, his violin is not much mentioned.

When Halley's Comet* puts in one of its rare appearances – it orbits approximately every seventy-five years – Alfgar rides his bike up a local hill several times in a bid to see it. He calls the comet 'the Beast', probably because there's a public panic going on. An astronomer has made lurid predictions about how gases in the comet's tail are a possible threat to life. Sales of gas masks, bogus 'anti-comet' pills and umbrellas are booming.

This is an exciting time for a young engineer. The great ship *Titanic* is being built, and motorcars are reaching the mighty speed of twelve miles per hour by the year 1912. Horse-drawn trams are giving way to motorised models.

The 1911 census sees Alice and Alfgar living at 3 Hawarden Terrace in Abergavenny. He's listed as an assistant colliery engineer aged twenty-three. Alice, then forty-six, is described as a 'widow of private means', so it seems she does have an income. However, she doesn't sound well. 'Mother bad. Nervous prostration',† he writes on 14 January. The next day, again, 'Mother bad.' But a week later, 'better'.

Nervous prostration was a term used to describe extreme mental and physical fatigue caused by high emotional stress. Multiple symptoms included exhaustion, sleeplessness, worry and low mood. Today we can take antidepressants. Back then you retreated to your bed. Life with Alice was probably not much fun.

Close to two years after Eric's departure, Alfgar is still in touch

---

* Halley's Comet, https://en.wikipedia.org/wiki/Halley%27s_Comet
† Nervous prostration, https://medical-dictionary.thefreedictionary.com/nervous+prostration

with his younger brother. 'Sent card to Eric,' he writes on 29 January 1911. And Alice is still seeing her own family. In April, Alfgar writes: 'Saw M off to Walsall', his mother's hometown.

He 'mooched about' but is mostly busy down the pit or swotting, seeing friends, dancing, taking golf lessons, going to church and attending evening lectures on such topics as 'Ancient Man' and 'The Mimicry of Animals'.

In 1913 Alfgar is still coping with Alice's ill health, noting several weeks of January misery two years after her previous bout. His mother is very ill with a 'bad attack' on 4 January. It is more than three weeks before he can scribble, 'Mother sat up twice, for half an hour!' And another week before he writes, 'Mother out first time.'

In his early twenties prior to World War 1, Alfgar, now an engineer, lived with his mother in Wales and coped with her frequent bouts of 'nervous prostration'. Photo: Nick Frost collection

No wonder Alfgar is keen to get out and enjoy life with friends. He reports on a 'jolly' cricket dance at Tredegar, from which he comes home at 4.30am.

He wants to look dapper for social occasions, carefully noting in his diary the details he needs for the ordering of clothes: Height, five foot ten and a half inches (1.8m); weight, eleven stone six pounds (72.6kg); hat, seven and one-eighth.

Meanwhile, where was Eric? Very far away. In his 1909 diary, Alfgar noted his new address – in the care of a Mrs Adams at 298 Isabel St, Winnipeg.

I didn't know who had sent him away, and why. Was it a case of the family quietly getting rid of Eric from their circle? Or, aware that he would never truly belong, did Eric himself decide that emigration was what he wanted – a chance for a fresh start in a new land, free from doubts and whispers?

I thought I'd never find out when he left England, but a librarian at the New Zealand Maritime Museum in Auckland suggested I try searching passenger lists in the UK's national archives.*

I soon found his name in a long list of children who sailed from Liverpool to Quebec as steerage passengers on a ship called the *Corsican* in May 1909. Eric Thompson was sixteen, but many of the solo youngsters weren't even twelve.

No middle names were included, so was this the right Eric? The ship sailed just a week after Alfgar's note saying 'Eric departed'. Thousands of boys and girls were being loaded onto Atlantic ships then. Canada wanted to boost its population and for many years ran a massive juvenile immigration scheme.

---

* British passenger lists, www.nationalarchives.gov.uk

As I looked down the passenger list, the old-fashioned names of all those children tugged at my heart. Such a Victorian crowd they were. The boys had names like Alfred, Harold, Fred, Cecil and Sidney. Girls were often Ada, Edith, Bertha, Ethel and Nellie.

It sounds like a grim passage. The Catholic Emigration Society instructed British medical officers to check for a huge range of childhood ailments, such as rickets, knock-knee, discharging ears, conjunctivitis and scabies, and the children were subjected to more examinations on arrival.

Doctors needed to watch out for 'nervous diseases' too – hallucinations, delusions or melancholia – and had to bear in mind the 'excitement induced through fear, grief and the experience of surrounds strange to them'. If they failed to impress Canadian officials, they could be deported back to where they'd come from – and that, one Catholic group pointedly commented, caused 'annoyance and waste of money'.

Agents accompanied the children. They had to sleep in the youngsters' quarters too. 'Children should never be left without someone in charge.' Their first, rather alarming, duty was to take care that none of them fell from the deck into the hold. Each day they had to ensure their charges washed before breakfast. Every second day 'they should be made to wash thoroughly stripped to the waist'. Girls' hair had to be fine-combed twice a day.

Each child was inspected to ensure they undressed before sleeping. And once in bed, they had to keep silent. There was lots of praying – grace before and after meals, plus morning and night prayers – though not after 9.30pm. The agents read prayers for

Sunday Mass, and said the Rosary on Sunday afternoons. Good behaviour and tidiness was essential, with agents always watching that no clothing was ever left on deck.

It was also their duty to 'parade all the childen with bare arms for doctor's examination of vaccination, at the time and on a day fixed by the doctor.' This was for smallpox – children had to have been vaccinated within the previous twelve months.

Eric may well have resented being herded and disciplined but would have had no option but to fall into line.

An estimated one hundred thousand youngsters crossed the Atlantic to settle in Canada between 1869 and 1948. The website of the British Isles Family History Society of Greater Ottawa[*] says the scheme was partly for the benefit of families whose own children had grown up – 'empty-nesters who missed the sound of children in their homes or for families who wanted children but had none of their own'. If children were fourteen years or older when they arrived, they had to receive wages while they learned a skill that would make them a living as adults.[†] Of course the youngsters were, chiefly, a source of cheap labour. Some had a miserable time, ending up with people who ill-treated or abused them.

Mrs Adams was one of many women who took in British youngsters like Eric. They were known as 'Home Children' and Canada wanted them to help fill their huge country and become future

---

[*] Canadian Library and Archives, https://www.bac-lac.gc.ca/eng/discover/immigration/immigration-records/home-children-1869-1930/Pages/home-children.aspx
[†] US military archives, www.fold3.com

useful citizens. Many households wanted a girl who could be trained in domestic skills or a boy strong enough to tackle farm chores. Some teens were apprenticed in trades that ranged from hat-making to telegraphy and machinery repair. Eric must have got to grips with book-keeping at some point, for that was his job for the rest of his life.

The Home Children were Britain's less fortunate youngsters – workhouse kids, orphans, the offspring of single parents, or those who came from homes where normal family life wasn't sustainable.

As a widow's son, Eric's situation ticked at least one of those boxes. While the Thompsons and the Hampsons were well heeled, Alice might have struggled financially on her own. Given Eric's awkward fit in the Thompson family, it is plausible that a one-way voyage to Montreal was seen as a good solution to the what-to-do-with-Eric dilemma.

I was still doubtful that the Eric amongst the crowd on board the *Corsican* was the right one. However, as I kept hunting for him online, I eventually found proof it was indeed Eric, for on a site devoted to Canada–US border crossings, there he was. Only now it was 1916, seven years later.

A US customs card recorded the arrival of New Zealand-born Eric Thompson, book-keeper, in his early twenties, in Detroit. It said he had first arrived in Quebec in 1909 on the *Corsican*. At his 1916 border crossing into America, he claimed he had no Canadian relatives or friends and was carrying $50 in cash. He was slightly shorter than Alfgar at five foot eight inches tall (1.78m), had brown hair, a medium complexion and no medical conditions.

His age was put down as twenty-two, but he was really twenty-four. After he left England, his birth year was out by two years in every official record I found. Even his death certificate would say he was born in 1894 when it was really 1892.

For some reason Eric fibbed about his age his whole adult life. The emigration authorities noted he was sixteen when he first went to Canada, but most of his *Corsican* shipmates were no more than fourteen and even as young as seven. The boy who'd always struggled to fit in may have called himself fourteen to get along more easily with the other children. And if that pretence suited him, it was easy to keep it up. After that it became a habit.

WHERE HAD HE BEEN, I wondered, between his first Canadian arrival in 1909 and the border crossing of 1916? It was all a mystery. The Thompson family who'd been at the centre of the old 'Waikomiti murder mystery' had faded to nothing. There was no one left to tell their tale now except me, an unconnected stranger who was becoming ever more obsessed with their story.

The online genealogy database business was in its infancy twenty years ago when Carolyn's contact, Monica Leat, was doing her research. It's easier now. Today, millions of people are looking for family histories. It's a massive enterprise, with billions of records available to anyone willing to pay membership money and start looking.

In I dived, and quickly found how gripping ancestry searching can be, even when you're not seeking your own forebears. The Thompsons were becoming so real to me. My heart ached for each of them in turn – for William with his crumbling marriage and unfulfilled rural dreams, and Alice with her own unhappiness, all too ready to fall for a dangerous newcomer... and the terrible consequences of her choice. Their two sons had been left fatherless – Alfgar apparently thriving, but Eric exiled far from home. As I kept delving, I began to think he was the survivor worst affected by what had happened when he was just a few weeks old.

I was soon knee-deep in online searching, spending countless hours on such sites as ancestry.com, myheritage.com, findmypast.com, familysearch.org and findagrave.com.

CHAPTER TWENTY-NINE

We'll never know how well Eric got on in the Adams house. He might not have been easy to handle. His background of exclusion could have made him a touchy kind of kid. Maybe he hated Winnipeg's brutal winter cold – there are few days between November and March when the temperature rises above freezing. Or perhaps he could see brighter horizons in the United States.

I did a lot of futile searching for him in Canadian records, where he seemed to sink into oblivion. The 1916 border-crossing form he'd filled in when in his early twenties indicated he already knew people in Detroit, because he wrote down a local address.

It was a golden city then, the centre of America's booming vehicle business. Henry Ford's black Model T cars were rolling off the assembly line. Customers couldn't get enough of them and work must have been plentiful. Detroit was bursting with potential for a lonely young man then.

Meanwhile, World War I was thundering along in Europe and his elder brother Alfgar had already been a soldier for two years, quickly promoted to sergeant and then to officer status. Nick Frost's cardboard box contained a handsome document dated 19 April 1916, which in flowing calligraphy and flowery language appointed Alfgar as an officer in King George V's land forces. Soon he was moving on to the Tank Corps. Tanks were an astonishing and novel idea back then, still very much in the trial stages. Alfgar's mechanical skills were most useful.

Alfgar at his desk as 'OC Experiments' in World War I working on early tank warfare. Photo: Nick Frost collection

Winston Churchill, then First Lord of the Admiralty, wanted the army to be equipped with a machine that could plough through mud and crunch right over the top of enemy barbed wire and trenches. The idea was that tanks would lead the charge, with infantry soldiers following on behind to finish the fighting on foot. Alfgar was stationed at a base called Bovington in Dorset, still used by the British Army today. A photo in an old family album shows him seated behind a desk with telephone at hand and boxes jammed full of papers. He has scrawled a caption underneath, labelling himself 'OC experiments' – OC standing for Officer Commanding. I thought he was making a joke until I found a war record saying he did do experimental work.

Churchill had set up a group called the Landships Committee. They put the boffins to work, and the first use of tanks was in the Battle of the Somme in September 1916. Heavy and slow, and apparently dreadful to ride in, they often got bogged down.

They did, however, terrify the first enemy soldiers who saw them coming. A story on the Bovington Tank Museum's site tells how someone yelled in panic that a crocodile was crawling into the German lines. 'The poor wretch was off his head. He had seen a tank for the first time and had imagined this giant of a machine, rearing up and dipping down as it came on, to be a monster ...'*

THE UNITED STATES finally declared war on Germany in April 1917, and Eric's draft registration card was recorded in June. The American paperwork was brisk and efficient. No fancy calligraphy for Eric. He supplied, as usual, a birth year two years later than his actual year of birth. He was really twenty-five, but told the army twenty-three. A clerk scribbled down his height (medium), his build (slight), his eye colour (light blue), hair (dark brown) and wrote 'no' in the box that asked if he was bald.

There was a section in which he could name grounds to claim exemption from service. He gave it a go with 'bad knee'. This was apparently ignored because in July of 1918 Private Eric

---

* British tank history, https://archaeology-travel.com/england/the-history-of-tanks-at-the-bovington-tank-museum/

Thompson was aboard the *Mauretania*, a once-elegant passenger liner turned troop ship, heading across the Atlantic. He was destined for Headquarters Company 328 Field Artillery, 8th Division.

There wasn't much of the war left to run; it ended four months later, but Eric was still in France early in 1919. Proof comes from a studio photo of him in uniform, taken on 1 January in a town called Saumur in the Loire Valley, where the US Army had a training base. All armies need admin staff, so he was probably doing accounting for the military. Trim and handsome, he gazes seriously into the camera. He wrote on the back: 'To my darling mother, with love from Eric.' Somehow, the picture ended up in Nick Frost's attic and came to me more than a century later, sepia tinged, in the cardboard box of random Thompson items.

It's the only evidence there is for an enduring relationship between mother and son. If they wrote to each other in Eric's American years, none of the correspondence survives. Possibly Alice never saw the photo. In April of 1919, only four months after it was taken, she died at St Elizabeth's Convent in Walthamstow, London. It was almost exactly ten years after Eric had left England.

Nick Frost was told by his aunt Hester that Eric had made a return visit to Burton-on-Trent soon after the war ended. I'm guessing this would have been his first visit back to the Thompson family estate since leaving in 1909.

Eric had just lost Alice, and Hester's mother was grieving for a brother who had died of an illness he'd contracted while away at war. Eric had leave for a while, but on 9 June 1919, according to ancestry.com, he was finally heading back to the States aboard the USS *Martha Washington*.

When I first sighted Eric's photo with its loving signature, I saw him as a young, single soldier. I wonder if, when he visited Burton-on-Trent in 1919, he gave other family members that impression too. But in my internet trawling I was surprised to discover that only a month after signing his army draft card, Eric had married for the first time, on 28 July 1917.

His bride was a nineteen-year-old New Yorker, Ruth Hagorlome. Many young people rushed into marriages then, grabbing happiness before the war rolled over them. They weren't together for long. Eric was called up a few months later – and apparently never came back. There can't have been much happiness at all. Ruth divorced him in 1920, citing extreme cruelty, non-support and desertion. The divorce record shows he did not contest it.

Eric had this 1919 French studio photo taken of himself in US Army uniform, and wrote a loving message to his mother on its back. Photo: Nick Frost collection

Those grounds sound grim, but cruelty was a common reason given for American couples to part.* It was a way for aggrieved spouses to assert that their marriage was too awful to continue. It did not necessarily mean physical abuse, but indicated 'conduct that causes embarrassment, humiliation and anguish so as to

---

* Cruelty as grounds for divorce, https://legal-dictionary.thefreedictionary.com/Mental+Cruelty

render life miserable and unendurable, or to cause a spouse's life, person or health to become endangered'.

Their divorce was one of fifteen detailed on the same page in Michigan archives, and nearly all of them included cruelty as at least one cause of those marriage splits. Divorces soared in the post-war years as servicemen struggled to adjust to civilian life and wives found absence didn't always make the heart grow fonder. By 1920, Eric had been gone for two years. Ruth must have tired of waiting for him.

It seems he already felt distant from his young wife as he set off for war. In US military archives* there's a record of his departure. Each man could write down the name of someone to contact in an emergency. In effect, the army was asking *if you die or are wounded, who do we write to?* There are twenty-five other soldiers' names on Eric's page, with an accompanying list of wives, fathers, mothers, siblings. There was not a single loved one whom Eric cared to mention. Instead there was just an 'Oliver Crew, friend', who lived in Detroit.

He had to give a family member's name again when he was shipped back to the States in 1919. That time he chose Alice Thompson, his mother, as the one to receive any bad news. He gave her address as Lyme Regis, Dorset. This was odd, as when his ship left port she'd already been two months in her grave. The existence of his wife, Ruth, was once again ignored. I wondered why he'd have given his dead mother's details, but he could have been required to supply an address well ahead of embarkation, when Alice was still alive.

---

* US military archives, www.fold3.com

CHAPTER THIRTY

Once divorced from Ruth in October 1920, Eric was quick to try marriage again. Only two months later he swapped 'I do' vows with a Detroit saleslady, Olive Haugh. She appears in the 1920 US census, living as a homeowner with two 'roomers'. Eric's name is in that same census. He was lodging at a different address and doing the books for a radiator company.

I drew a blank in finding any more clues about them but then spotted a genealogy file I'd not opened before. It contained passport application forms from late in 1920 – and there was Eric again.

He wanted to go overseas on vacation – well, actually on honeymoon – and had to tell the US government a lot about himself. He declared he had arrived in the US on 15 June 1910 and had 'lived in Detroit uninterruptedly' for the next decade.

Wait, *what?* That date floored me. It meant that only a year after leaving England at sixteen in 1909, Eric had abandoned Canada and pushed on to Detroit, more than a thousand miles from Winnipeg. And it meant the 1916 border-crossing card I'd seen earlier was a much later entry into the United States.

He had only just become a naturalised US citizen when he applied for the joint passport for himself and Olive. A married woman was then just a footnote on the application, referred to merely as 'and wife'. (It would be the late 1930s before American women could get separate passports issued in their own names.)

There's a photo of the dark-haired pair side by side, looking solemn. He noted they were going on a post-wedding trip to France to visit friends, and to England to see relatives. I wonder if he took her to meet his brother.

His recent citizenship status was intriguing because he'd already been a US soldier. Almost eighteen per cent of men in the US Army in World War I were foreign-born. One New York City army unit was so full of immigrants they nicknamed it 'the Melting Pot Division'. Some became naturalised while in uniform, and then new laws were enacted after the war to speed the process for more veterans who wanted citizenship. Eventually, more than three hundred thousand people became Americans this way, including Eric.*

He and Olive were away four months, arriving back at Ellis Island, New York, the following April – so it was a long honeymoon. Both of them were listed then as twenty-eight years old, which was wrong on both counts, as he was twenty-nine and she about eight years older, depending on which birth record you rely. Olive had

---

* Naturalisation of US soldiers, https://www.uscis.gov/about-us/our-history/history-office-and-library/featured-stories-from-the-uscis-history-office-and-library/the-immigrant-army-immigrant-service-members-in-world-war-i

been married before, too. Her divorce listing says it was yet another extreme-cruelty case.

Perhaps the honeymoon was a healing experience for two wounded souls. They sailed in the *Old North State*, which had sixty-four cabins – all designated first class. Eric had travelled to Canada in steerage in 1909 and in a cramped troop ship to Europe during the war. This time he must have wanted classier accommodation.

Meanwhile, elder brother Alfgar was thriving. He worked for the French motor company, Citroën, and had a support role in a grand expedition – the first motorised crossing of the Sahara Desert, in 1922. Special trucks were built for the job, with wheels at the front and tank tracks at the rear for pushing up and over sand dunes. Alfgar's experience in tank design would have equipped him well for the job. A team of French adventurers succeeded, with a white dog called Flossie as their mascot. In the foreword to a book called *Across the Sahara by Motorcar*, company founder Andre Citroën wrote: 'The hum of our motors has a beauty of its own. It is the song of progress, the rhythm of human effort chanting its victory over the elements.'

No such romance for Eric in Detroit, where he kept on book-keeping. Census records reveal no children. There's also no knowing whether the brothers kept in touch during or after the war, though Alfgar had also married in the spring of 1917. That was just three months before Eric's first nuptials. I wondered when I compared the dates if Eric heard of his brother's wedding and thought he too should marry, and young Ruth was there to step into his arms.

A photo of Alfgar and his bride, a nurse named Phyllis Morris, shows their smiling exit through the doors of St Jude's Church in Kensington, London – Alfgar in uniform with his officer's cap and swagger stick and Phyllis in a satin coat-dress with roses tucked under its sash and a broad-brimmed hat. He looks about to burst with happiness. Phyllis was modern and lively. Family photos show her astride a motorcycle, her grin a mile wide, dressed for country pursuits.

Alfgar and Phyllis Thompson, full of smiles at their 1917 London wedding. Photo: Nick Frost collection

In one faded snapshot from a family album, the pair are sitting together on a doorstep. It was taken when they first fell in love. They look very contented. A scribbled caption underneath says,

'Here beginneth – us'. They would later have two daughters. Margaret Eileen (called Eileen by the family) arrived in 1919 and Alison in 1925. For a few years, life was lovely.

Alfgar's past had been marred by the early deaths of his poisoned father and his cancer-stricken older brother, Alaric. Both were gone from his life when he was so young he never knew them. But the next time tragedy came to call, it was agonising.

Alfgar's first-born Eileen on her mother's knee in a 1920s portrait. Photo: Nick Frost collection

In the bundle of Thompson papers there was an extra, elegant little diary for 1926. It was a memento from the Hotel Continental Paris. Alfgar was no doubt often in France on business, so was probably a regular guest. The printed flyleaf wishes him a Merry Christmas and a Happy New Year.

He was thirty-seven by then, a family man living in leafy Richmond, Surrey. His diary entries reveal tennis, gardening, houseboating, dancing lessons and socialising as well as work events. He mentions often being at Citroën's Slough factory close to London. The site is long gone, but thousands of French vehicles were once built there. In the 1920s Citroën had an assembly plant there and he wrote down reminders of company dances and lunches. In October of 1926 he visited Walsall and saw his aunt Lizzie, Alice's sister. So, seven years after his mother's death, he was still connected to her side of the family. Every day of that autumn is filled with his tiny writing until 8 November, when it comes to a jolting stop. He writes diagonally across an otherwise blank page 'Alison ill'. The next ten days' pages are also empty, except for one cryptic note of the number 104. I wondered if that indicated his little girl had a raging fever – 104°F is a dangerously high temperature in a toddler. Then, on 28 November, he puts just two sad words: 'Alison died.' She was just a little tot – only twenty months old.

I ordered up her death certificate. It cited pneumonia. Poor Alison. Too sick, too early. The penicillin that might have saved her would not go into mass production for another fifteen years.

Now Alfgar and Phyllis had only their elder daughter, Eileen, who features in many black-and-white family snaps. She's there as a baby in her father's arms. Doting Alfgar has a rifle over one shoulder and his daughter in the crook of the other arm. Later, she's a smiling little girl with dark eyes and glossy fringe, perched alongside her dad as he puffs on his pipe. He had a pet name for her, Whiskers, revealed in a few yellowing undated notes, full of love and humour.

Countryman Alfgar with gun and pipe and little Eileen for company. He fondly called her Whiskers. Photo: Nick Frost collection

Eileen went on a summer holiday to Bognor with her mother and wrote a brief letter to Alfgar, who had stayed at home. 'My darling Daddy,' she starts off and then teases him for his penmanship. 'I think you might have chosen a larger piece of paper and done larger writing, because I could hardly see the paper and I strained my eyes badly trying to read your writing!'

He must have sent a cheeky sketch of her and she says she won't 'retaliate' due to her lack of artistic skill. 'There is nothing like being really polite to your self-like daughter about her little red pants,' she jokes, not quite getting 'sylph-like' right. At the end, Eileen includes 'love from Mummy' and adds a cheerful 'Toodle-oo! Your loving Whiskers.'

How heartbreaking it was for Alfgar and Phyllis when she too fell ill and died at only seventeen in 1935. Once again, I ordered a death certificate.

Back in 1891, Alfgar's older brother Alaric had died of kidney cancer. Alfgar was only two then. More than forty years later, his girl Eileen also had kidney failure – but this time it resulted from an infection of the lining of her heart. In the 1920s they called it 'malignant endocarditis'. Doctors could have done nothing to save her.

Nick Frost's mother and Eileen had been childhood friends. When I told Nick about how Eileen had died, he said his own family still has reminders of her in the form of inherited silver cutlery with her initials, MET, engraved on the handles. 'We use them daily,' Nick told me. 'Hearing about her again is rather like being visited by spirits from the past.'

She died at home. Her death certificate says Alfgar was 'present at death'. Phyllis would have been there too, but is not mentioned.

Women were legally invisible in so many ways then. Phyllis does not even appear on her own first-born's birth certificate because it was not until the end of Eileen's birth year, 1919, that mothers' names were included in English Birth Index records.

Would Alfgar have written a sad note to Eric, his American brother, about Eileen's tragic death or had they drifted apart by then? After all, it was twenty-six years since Eric had left England.

By the time Eileen died in 1935, her uncle Eric was living in distant Millbrae, San Francisco. He was then a thirty-three-year-old credit manager for an optical lens firm. Perhaps he'd tired of Detroit and sought a balmier life on the west coast. It seemed that, like his mother, he kept moving about. The 1940 census shows Eric and Olive had shifted to sunny Los Angeles. Eric was earning $3800 a year, and they were paying $60 per month in rent. There were no children.

They'd been wed twenty years but were still not settled, and soon they were back up the coast again in 'Frisco. A 1942 World War II registration card puts him there aged forty-eight. That sounds old for military service, but the US government was contacting all American men aged between forty-five and fifty-five in case they might be useful to the war effort. Old soldiers had already been called up again in England, and Alfgar was back in uniform in his mid-fifties. Now ranked Major Thompson, his job was 'Principal Inspector of Armaments Gauges'. In San Francisco, Eric was asked for 'the name of the person who will always know your address'. He wrote 'Olive Thompson', but oddly, her address was different from his own. Why were they living apart? What did that say about their marriage?

CHAPTER THIRTY-ONE

THE THOMPSON BROTHERS' TRAGEDIES AND TRIALS IN THE years before World War II meant nothing to Alice, for she died just after World War I. And given her dire marital history she'd have hardly have been qualified to offer relationship advice to her sons. Widowed at only twenty-seven, she stayed single for the rest of her rather short life. She died on 3 April 1919, aged fifty-four, just as Alfgar's first daughter, Eileen (Alice's first grandchild), was entering the world. Alfgar would have been torn between the funeral and the birth.

I'm hoping he chose to be with Phyllis. Alice was, anyway, safe in a world of women when she passed away. Monica Leat, researching her story twenty years before me, had found that Alice died in the Catholic convent of St Elizabeth's in London. Unable to find any records, Monica didn't know if she worked at the convent (which was also a school) or had taken refuge there.

Monica had also found her grave and taken a photo of the small stone cross that stands on it. Carolyn has it in her files. As I studied it, I noticed a strange thing. Fungus and moss have spread across the name carved on the cross, so it's hard to read. But when I enlarged the picture, I could just make out five extra letters.

At some stage Alice acquired another name. She had started out in life with two first names – Sarah Alice, and they were still that way when she signed the probate form after William's death in 1892. But by the end of her life in 1919 she had added Paula. Sarah Alice Paula. What was *that* about?

Perhaps she felt guilty all her life, for even if Scott did not conspire with her to murder William and acted alone – or even if William actually took his own life – the awful drama on Parker Road would not have taken place without her part in it. In midlife she may have yearned to withdraw from the world and find forgiveness – and a nunnery could deliver those things. She'd grown up Anglican, but Alice must have leaned towards a different faith as she grew older.

I knew of no Catholic connection to the Paula name, but it didn't take long to discover St Paula, patron saint of widows. Ah-ha, I thought. In twenty-seven years of widowhood, Alice had spent a lot of time alone. Maybe she felt drawn to the story of St Paula, a young noblewoman of ancient Rome who became deeply Christian after the death of her husband.

He'd been wealthy. Paula was used to being carried through the city by eunuch slaves. No doubt she hosted brilliant, rowdy dinners where good wine and conversation flowed, the food was splendid and she wore beautiful jewels.

An online *Vatican News** story about St Paula says she was the wife of a senator.

When he died she changed her life, joining a group of Christian widows who devoted themselves to penance and prayer. She turned her 'great Roman house' over to them. With her glamorous guests gone, the rooms filled instead with quiet prayer and song.

---

* *Vatican News*, www.vaticannews.va

CHAPTER THIRTY-TWO

It makes sense that Alice found comfort in being one of many women throughout history who have sought solace in retreat. Eventually I learnt her Catholic connection must have gone back a decade or more before she died.

I'd puzzled over whether Eric was sent to Canada in 1909, or had wanted to go. When I found him in a ship's passenger list amongst a crowd of kids in steerage, I'd assumed he was one of Canada's Home Children. But the more I read about them, the more he seemed an odd fit. Most were street kids, workhouse children, orphans and the like. Some were totally destitute and were often described as forlorn waifs and strays. One article in a Catholic publication said 'the emigrant boy, as a rule, is originally taken from the gutter of our great cities … Drunkenness, foul language, immorality, want and cruelty have been familiar to him from infancy.'

Given the prosperity in Eric's background, it seemed strange that he was parcelled up with youngsters from such awful situations.

Maybe it meant Alice was just scraping by. Census records usually say she had 'private means', which *sounds* comfortable. But maybe she was desperate. Maybe she just couldn't cope.

I had previously browsed for information about Eric without success on a site run by the British Isles Family History Society of Greater Ottawa.* When I went back in to try one more time, I sent off an email asking for help, thinking I'd be lucky to hear anything back. Some museums and libraries I'd approached took days or weeks to reply, but just two hours later there was fresh Eric news in my inbox. They had him on file! And yes, he *was* one of the Home Children.

He'd been scooped up in a project headed by a Father George Hudson, a Catholic priest apparently devoted to care of homeless children. Hudson himself sometimes crossed the Atlantic with groups of young emigrants. It was a nine-day voyage, followed by a twelve-hour train trip to Ottawa.

The Thompson family were staunch Church of England. Alice grew up Anglican too. Her conversion must have taken place before Eric left England, as it's unlikely he'd have been included in the Catholic party unless he was nominally Catholic too.

In 1905 Hudson had established a large receiving house for boys (and later girls) in Ottawa. The brick building still stands as a parish office, but its initial name was the St George's Receiving Home.† Ten thousand of them, including Eric, came through its doors in its early years. As each batch arrived, they had days of

---

* British Isles Family History Society of Greater Ottawa, https://www.bifhsgo.ca/
† Father Hudson, https://britishhomechild.com/st-georges-receiving-home-in-ottawa

instruction on what to expect before being sent to their new homes.

The Adams house in Winnipeg was Eric's destination. And I learnt a little about that too. Paul Adams, a fireman at 'Number 3 Fire Hall', is listed in *Peel's Prairie Provinces Winnipeg City Directory 1910* as head of the household at 298 Isabel Street. That was the address Alfgar had jotted in his worn leather diary. The export of Catholic children stopped in 1932, but Father Hudson's organisation is still an English social welfare agency based in Birmingham. It is now called Father Hudson's Care. A helpful Canadian volunteer gave me a contact for an English staffer who had access to Home Children records. It had been eight years since he was last in touch with her. She'd probably long since left the job, he said, but it was still worth trying. With fingers crossed I sent off an email to that very old address, hoping she was still around and that she could help.

'Yes, I'm still here!' she replied. Kindly, she went searching. Eric had left just a tiny trace in their files, but the staffer was able to give me a couple of new clues. He was registered as 'a private case', which was most unusual. She had rarely seen it in their records. 'I suspect that as a favour, the Catholic Emigration Society was asked if he could sail with their party.'

I imagine Alice knocking at her priest's door to ask if there was a way the church could arrange passage for Eric. They did. And in 1909 someone at the Hudson office had scribbled alongside his name 'Gone to friends'.

It meant there had been some kind of travel plan; Eric hadn't just been cast off into an unknown future. However, the 'friends' named Adams are a mystery. It's hard to imagine how a wealthy British brewing family and a Winnipeg fireman's household were connected. Maybe there was a link between the Adamses and someone in the Thompson household – a cook, housekeeper or gardener. The only tiny link to Canada I found in Alfgar's set of diaries was that one night in 1910 he played 'Canadian whist' with his granny and an aunt.

Eric was noted just once more in Hudson records. 'Off the books' was written alongside his name seven months after his arrival in Winnipeg. That meant he was no longer under Catholic care. I already knew that in 1910 he'd headed off more than 1600 kilometres away to Detroit.

Meanwhile, his elder brother Alfgar was hard at work in a Welsh colliery and would soon be writing in his diary about his mother's poor health, which continued to decline through that decade.

Alice's younger sister, Lizzie, was with her when she died in April 1919 of aortic valvular disease and angina pectoris. She had, as they would have said, a 'bad heart'. She left not much behind – £117 gross, equivalent to about £6000 today. The net amount, after expenses, came to a mere £63. Her will had been written in 1914, and she left everything to Alfgar with not a mention of Eric. If Alfgar died before her, she wanted her sister and brother-in-law to receive 'my Spode tea and coffee service, all my sterling silver articles and goods, and my mahogany case of plates and cutlery'. Ten pounds was to go to the priest in Caerphilly, near Cardiff, for the saying of masses for her soul, and any residue could be used by him for the Mission there.

She requested that she be interred according to the rites of the church, 'clothed in my Habit of the Third Order'. What was that? In those days it meant she was devout but not quite a nun. A helpful person at New Zealand's Catholic Enquiry Centre explained she would have been practising some of the spirituality of her Catholic order, without becoming professed as a member – so in law she was still a layperson.

The habit Alice mentioned was just a simple dark gown. Women's congregations often felt called to care for widows. While living in the convent, she'd have helped with domestic work and prayed with the sisters. The life offered 'a peaceful ending after sometimes brutal or unhappy lives', said my informant.

ALFGAR WOULD HARDLY HAVE NEEDED her china and cutlery. He would do well. When he died in 1957, his estate was valued at £21,131, worth more than half a million pounds in today's money. In New Zealand terms he was a millionaire.

By then he'd retired and the couple were living back at the Old Farm in Burton-on-Trent, where he'd spent much of his boyhood. After Alfgar passed away, the Old Farm went to his widow, Phyllis. Nick Frost did not know Alfgar, who died before he was born, but does remember Phyllis, whom he called Aunty Phyl. 'She was a grandmother-like figure to me,' he told me. The young Phyllis who had loved outdoor sports and motorcycle riding was old by the time he knew her.

'I would be allowed to choose a present from a toy shop in Burton – usually a toy gun, to Phyllis's dismay. I remember her being very deaf and shuffling around on a Zimmer frame. She had a cosy living room and we would sit on the sofa together and talk about fishing.'

Aunty Phyl died in 1971 when Nick was ten. With both of her

daughters long dead, she had no heirs. She left the Old Farm to Nick's mother, playmate of Phyllis's elder girl, Eileen.

Phyllis also left funds to help with Nick's education. He visited the house often as a boy and still has a photo of a shield that hung in its hallway. It was from Balliol College at Oxford University – no doubt a souvenir of William Thompson's time there.

Phyllis was an active and sporty nurse who loved riding motorcycles in her youth. Photo: Nick Frost collection

CHAPTER THIRTY-THREE

I STARTED OUT KNOWING NOTHING OF ERIC'S LATER LIFE. I'D been told that neither Alfgar nor Eric had left direct descendants. It was such a shame, I'd thought, that there was no one left I could talk to. Alfgar's girls had died young, and as for Eric, well, he was a mystery, twice married but apparently childless. I had no idea what had happened to him, but when I unfolded some papers from the very bottom of Nick Frost's cardboard box, everything changed.

I was holding two fragile and yellowing letters from the Thompson family's lawyers, Drewry & Newbold, in Burton-on-Trent. Typewritten in May 1951, the notes are still pinned together with a rusting paperclip.

The firm had written to Alfgar to pass on sad news from attorneys in San Francisco. 'We regret to say we have received a letter this morning advising us that your brother, Mr E Thompson, passed away on April 3rd, and as his widow, Mrs Edith Thompson, does not appear to have your address, they ask us to notify you of the death of your brother.'

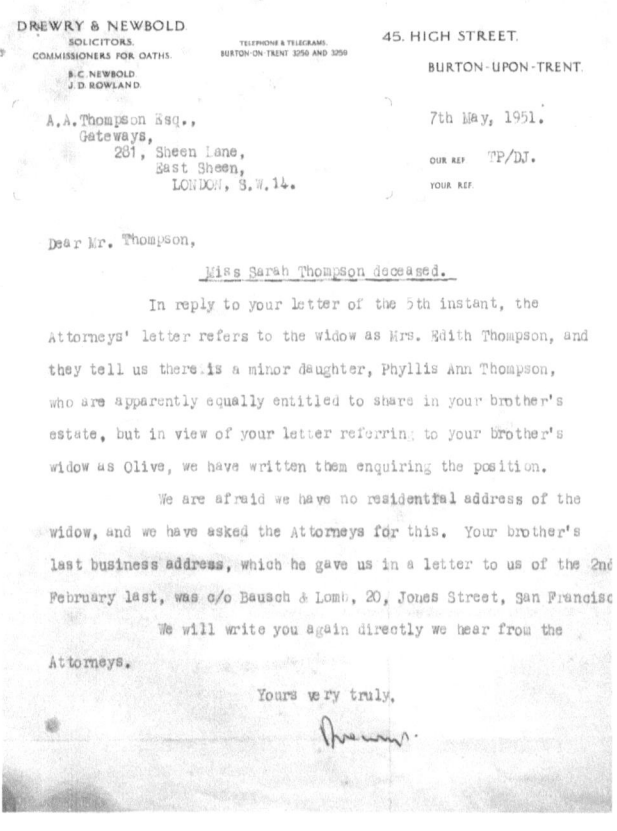

*Legal letter giving Alfgar surprise news that his late brother had a third wife – and a daughter, who, like Alfgar's wife, was also called Phyllis. Oddly, the 1951 letter is mistakenly headed with the name of a deceased Miss Sarah Thompson.
Image: Nick Frost collection*

So, Eric had died in his late fifties. But Edith? *Who was this?* I thought Eric was still married to Olive, who had honeymooned with him in Europe thirty years earlier and been with him for decades. This new wife was obviously a puzzle to Alfgar, too, for although his reply to the lawyers is missing, a second legal letter he received makes it clear he'd also thought Eric's widow was Olive. Instead he was learning there was not only another spouse, but also a daughter, and they were jointly entitled to share in Eric's estate.

I was astonished at the mention of a daughter. *Eric had had a child?* Amazing. There could be surviving family members! This news of a third wife pushed me online for the umpteenth time to see what else I could discover.

I was unable to find a divorce record for Eric and Olive, but when that marriage ended Eric had found a new bride. They wed in 1943. He was by then fifty, but his age was recorded as forty-eight. She was only twenty-nine. Olive had been some years older than Eric; now he had a much younger love. Edith was a secretary in the same business he worked in. An office romance, I reckon, that turned into something deeper.

I wish I could know how he felt two years later when Edith told him she was pregnant. Had he ever dreamed of fatherhood? Was he shocked? Nervous? Delighted? He was going to be quite an old first-time dad. I like to think the arrival of a tiny girl in 1945 brought him unexpected joy. He'd had little enough of that in his life. They called her Phyllis – it's possible she was named after Alfgar's Phyllis in England, Eric's sister-in-law. But if so, surely Eric would have written to his brother about it, but Alfgar didn't even know Eric *had* another wife, or a child.

I felt bad for Olive. It must have been hard for her, after a long and childless marriage, to learn she'd been supplanted by a much younger woman, who'd then had a baby. Ancestry.com told me Olive outlived Eric by twelve years and worked as a housekeeper, and that she died in Pennsylvania in 1963, at seventy-seven.

FindaGrave.com, which is a vast collection of burial sites, gave me more clues. A distant relative had set up a memorial page for Olive. It said that after her first divorce, Olive had married a younger man who had later left her for a much younger woman. That had to have been Eric. I messaged the writer of that note. 'Do you know anything else about her?' I asked. Very little, she said, but she did supply a strange snippet of news – that Olive was known all her life as Dollie.

How curious that Eric had once loved a woman whose nickname matched the one given his mother, Alice, by her lover. Well, almost the same – only the spelling is different.

I wonder if Eric ever knew in his twenty-two-year marriage to 'Dollie' that the same name was often whispered in his mother's ear by Alexander Scott, who may or may not have murdered Eric's father, or *been* his father.

It's easy to think of Eric as having been on the outer, but he wasn't forgotten. He's in a 1920 Thompson family pamphlet as one of dozens of cousins who served in World War I. His name also appears on a Thompson family tomb at Burton-on-Trent, though his remains are not there. Instead, he is buried in San Francisco. As a former US soldier he earned his place in a vast, quiet, military cemetery where clean white tombstones stand in lines on well-tended green grass. His third wife, Edith, lies there too. I found a picture of it on the 3foldflag.com website.

Eric's stone is inscribed with his name, rank and World War I unit, and his dates of birth and death. As usual, it says he was born in

1894, two years later than his actual birth. His death from a heart attack on 3 April 1951 was the same day on which his mother Alice had died, also of heart disease, thirty-two years earlier.

His inaccurate birth year made me think of little Alaric's headstone in Ōrātia Cemetery, half a world away, with his year of death wrong and his name mistakenly written as Aldric. His brother Eric's stone, with its wrong birthdate, was erected far across the Pacific about sixty years later. Even headstones, it seems, can't be trusted.

Having laid flowers on William's grave, I very much wanted to cross the ocean and put fresh blooms on Eric's resting place. It felt like no one else in the world remembered him and it seemed the least I could do. But Covid-19 meant long-haul travel ceased. I could only do it in my imagination.

I suspect Eric might not have liked me delving more into his life, but I wasn't quite done. I remembered the handwritten note he'd clipped to his 1920 passport application and realised I might still be able to get an idea of his character. Once again, I approached graphologist Mike Maran. Once again, I told him nothing about the background of the person whose writing I'd supplied.

The report's opening sentence said: 'Eric is bound up with retaining as many material possessions as he is able; not so much because he is greedy or materialistic, but because owning 'things' makes him feel safer.'

That made sense to me. Eric's boyhood was probably always one of comparing his brother Alfgar's comfortable life at Burton-on-Trent with the more tenuous one he had with Alice. No wonder he was motivated by a desire for safety.

Added Maran: 'He suffers from a low level of self-confidence ... his ego was trampled on at a young age and has not fully recovered. Consequently, he projects an embellished image of pride. Something has hampered the development of his self-esteem.' Oh yes, I thought, Eric must have felt 'other' all through his childhood. A feeling of being looked at askance and having never fitted in would undermine any young man's sense of self-worth.

The report also said: 'He is uptight and anxious much of the time. Eric needs positive feedback from others about his performance or he feels he is not 'ok'. His moods and responses change from moment to moment, going from high to low and back up again.'

In a paragraph headed 'red flags', the report said: 'Eric is sure that others are saying nasty things about him. In response, he goes on the offensive, making a pre-emptive strike before someone else can attack.'

Of course, people probably often *did* say nasty things about the awful story of his poor, dead dad and how his mother, Alice, had betrayed him. It's likely Alice was never free of tongue-wagging in places where her history was known. Eric would have been aware of the talk and borne the brunt of it too. Grown-ups often think that children aren't listening when secrets are whispered. But they are – and gossip can cause deep wounds.

It's good to read, though, that Eric had courage. 'Even when the going gets really tough and he finds himself filled with inner turmoil, he refuses to give in to feelings of despair or hopelessness. He calls on his reserves of strength for support.'

Maran noted Eric was logical and rational, which makes sense of his work as a book-keeper and credit manager. On the other hand, the handwriting indicated he struggled to respond to emotional situations. 'It is very difficult for him to let go of a relationship as his self-image is intricately bound up with how his partner sees him. The end of an affair is probably more devastating to him than anything else in life.'

Whether or not all of that assessment is accurate, I imagine he always sought what was missing in childhood – stability, self-respect and a constant supply of love. What he'd got was a mother whose own life was blighted, a brother whom he rarely saw, and an extended family who may or may not have shown him genuine encouragement and kindness.

Although he was blameless in the awful business of William's death, there would always have been those tiny seeds of doubt in aunts' and uncles' minds about who had fathered him.

And yet he wasn't entirely cut off. When Alfgar heard from the lawyers about his brother's death in 1951, the firm also advised they had recently sent to Eric's Californian bank account the proceeds of a sale of £500 worth of brewery shares, and that by now it should have arrived.

So, just over four decades after Eric had steamed out of Liverpool, he was still receiving money from Burton-on-Trent. By then the Pacific Division credit manager for Bausch & Lomb, and well settled with Edith ('beloved husband and devoted father', said his death notice), Eric had come a long way from the kid who'd jostled with the scared crowd of waifs and strays aboard the *Corsican*. How hard that must have been! One week he was in London being treated to a theatre outing with his big brother, the next he was pressed in amongst anxious strangers on the grey Atlantic, being shouted at and prayed over on the way to an unknown future.

Even though his parentage had been in doubt, I like to think of Eric as a Thompson. It was, after all, the name he carried all his life. And in the year Alice Thompson died, he still loved her enough to call her his darling mother on the back of a French studio photo, clearly meant as a gift to her.

CHAPTER THIRTY-FOUR

Alice's New Zealand love affair had killed her husband and wrecked her life. But she did have her boys, at least for a while. After Eric left for Canada, she still had Alfgar. As a young man he seems to have given her good care in her downtimes. And a final kind of blessing may have come from her last days in the company of nuns.

Old family-album photos of Alfgar with his family show there was happiness in his life – at least until illnesses ripped both his daughters away.

They say that if your life is in sudden peril, scenes from your past may swiftly spool through your mind. If that's true, then the collective 'film' of the Thompson family's lives from their New Zealand sojourn onwards would have been crammed with a blur of images. Horses and candlelight, kisses by a waterfall, a love letter, a spoonful of jam, and a hooded man trembling on a scaffold. Then there were all the sea voyages by steamship, troop ship and ocean liner – in first-class berths, army cots and cramped steerage bunks. Weddings, births and bereavements. Carriages and churches. Pessaries and poison. Laudanum and beer. Tanks. Warfare. Halley's Comet. Country life and cemeteries. Beloved dogs. Speeches and sadness. Violins and bones.

MOST OF THE dwellings where Thompson family members lived have gone. Eric's 1909 Winnipeg address is now occupied by a gas station. A freeway runs through one of his Detroit abodes, though I did find online a handsome old apartment building in central Los Angeles where he lived in 1940. The house he shared with Edith in Millbrae, San Francisco, is still there too.

The Burton-on-Trent homes where Alfgar lived as a boy are mostly gone, often demolished to make way for commercial buildings or higher-density housing. The Old Farm in Burton-on-Trent still exists, though the once open acres of garden and orchard around it are now heavily in-filled with modern housing. Nick Frost believes the house dates back to the sixteenth century. He played there as a boy and remembers a little headstone in the garden marking the spot where John Dog lay. Remember, Alfgar wrote in his 1906 diary about giving him a bath? He must have been well loved, that dog.

Another home that remains is the West Auckland one where the whole drama began, in Parker Road.

It is said to be the oldest wooden house in West Auckland and was built in the 1860s, two decades before William and Alice came to New Zealand. Archives New Zealand records show the property was granted to a man named Robert Ingram in 1864. It was part of a distribution of blocks of land administered by a body called the Office of the Waste Lands of Auckland. That unhappy title came about because the then government decided native title to the area had been 'extinguished' and the land was split into chunks for disposal.

Some of the house's internal planking was split by axe, then fastened with handmade nails. There are huge stone boulders in the ground below that act as foundations, still propping up some of the floor joists. There have been alterations over the years, of course – such as a kitchen extension and a repositioning of the staircase that accesses the upper floor under the roof.

The stairs up which Alice ran when policemen found incriminating evidence in Scott's trouser pocket the day after William's death. 'That's mine,' she cried. And yet she was never called to be a trial witness.

A deck and patio have been added to catch morning sun and there's a pool on the northern side. The room where William died has for many years been a bathroom, but the bones of the house that William and Alice knew as Sunnydale are much the same. Carolyn and Anthony use Alice's old bedroom today.

View out to the garden from the room where William died, which has long since been converted to a bathroom. Photos: Joey Tonks

It was Carolyn's girlhood home. Her parents, Dick and Annemarie Endt, bought it in 1962 from a family named Davidson. They found pages from 1864 *New Zealand Herald* issues lining some of the walls. Carolyn left home at eighteen, and about ten years later, when she married Anthony, they settled back there to bring up their three sons.

'I've lived in it pretty much all my life,' she says. 'We never thought of William's room as haunted, but it was always cold and had a kind of atmosphere.' That changed when she was contacted by Monica Leat and they did the research that opened up William's story twenty years ago. 'After that it felt lighter, as if we'd put things to rest and cleared the air.'

In the nineteenth century, the Ōrātia hills and valleys around bush-fringed Parker Road were mostly clad with tea tree and scrub, with settlers struggling to make their acreages useful for growing food – and, in William's case, apples. His own dream died with him, but there's lush growth on his old land today. It contains many rare botanical specimens, including marvellous palms that Carolyn's parents collected on long-ago travels in South America. It also became the base for a specialist nursery business, which the Mellings recently sold. They supplied fast-growing bamboo plants to householders eager for privacy in Auckland's increasingly crowded suburbs.

William Thompson, who yearned in his youth for wide open rural spaces, might have appreciated the slogan that went with their business logo – *No More Neighbours*.

THE THOMPSONS DIDN'T MAKE old bones. When Eric died in San Francisco in 1951, the only surviving member of his original family was his big brother, Alfgar, who would last only another six years.

Alice was gone at fifty-five, Eric at fifty-seven. Alfgar died of a brain haemorrhage at sixty-eight. William Thompson's dream of founding a family who would share his love of country life had crumbled to nothing.

But the tale wasn't yet quite told. After much online searching, I was blown away to discover Eric's daughter, Phyllis, was still alive and well in California. 'I've found her!' I trumpeted to Carolyn. I could hardly believe it. There she was – an actual surviving descendant of the Thompsons who'd once lived on Parker Road.

Eric's birth year of 1892 is so long ago that I'd assumed she was probably deceased. But no, it seemed she was still thriving in her seventies. But her existence rather unnerved me. How was I going to approach her?

By now I'd watched far too many episodes of TV shows like *Long Lost Family* and *Who Do You Think You Are?*, in which people search obsessively for ancestral stories and are, mostly, delighted by each new discovery.

I was hoping Eric's girl would feel the same way. She'd been hard to track down. At first all I had was a record of an early marriage in 1966, when she was just twenty-one. On the off chance, I dropped the groom's name into MyHeritage.com and found they'd attended the same San Francisco high school. Yearbook notes had described her as 'one of the school's finest dancers'. And sure enough, his little bio also said he enjoyed lunchtime dancing. High-school sweethearts, I concluded.

They divorced eleven years later. Carolyn and I both tried to find her through that first husband, who we discovered owned a California wine store. I tried calling it. No one picked up. I left a message, but never heard back. Carolyn even found his daughters on Facebook and messaged them, with no success. Of course their father's first wife was not connected with them at all, but I'd hoped they might have an idea of where Phyllis was and what her surname might now be. But we encountered only silence.

CHAPTER THIRTY-FIVE

Men are easier to track in a search like this. Their surnames stay constant, but when women marry and re-marry they become more elusive. But one day I somehow did something right on a genealogy site and the fact of Phyllis's second marriage was staring me in the face. In 1978 she had a new bridegroom, a man named John.

'Look at this!' I messaged Carolyn. When she searched for Phyllis under her married name, she quickly discovered fresh and contemporary photos of a silver-haired, smiling, elegant woman. The internet had previously only shown me a fuzzy photo of Phyllis from her 1962 high-school yearbook. How wonderful it was now to see her happy face in late life. It made me smile too. In one shot, she and John were dressed up for a party as the dour farming pair in the famous painting by Grant Ward, *American Gothic*. The farmer in that painting has a hayfork in hand. John was holding a rake instead and their expressions were mock-gloomy. I now knew they lived in Sonoma, north of San Francisco, and it was great to see they liked to have fun.

I fantasised about calling her – even flying to California to meet her. Maybe I could learn new things about her dad, Eric. She might have more photos or letters or intriguing old stories to tell. I even wondered if she might be willing to take a DNA test that might establish who Eric's father really was – William Thompson or Alexander Scott.

Then I came to my senses.

What right did I have to barge into her life? What if the things I knew about Eric's history would come as a huge shock? What if his background had been a family secret and she knew almost *nothing* about it? What if she didn't *want* to know.

How might she react to a distant stranger with possibly disturbing news about her father – not a distant ancestor but her actual dad.

In essence, I'd be saying, 'I'm keen to know whether your grandmother knew her lover wanted to get rid of her husband. Whether they actually plotted it together or if she was innocent. And whether your father was the son of the murder victim, or of the man who was hanged for poisoning him.'

No, I thought ... it was a step way too far. And yet, I'd been pushing on with the story for so long that I didn't want to stop now.

My approach was softly-softly. I'd been unable to find any more info about Phyllis online but did track down an email address for John – so I took a deep breath and sent off a request. His online information told me he'd been a police chief. A crime story might interest him, I thought, even if it was an old one from the bottom of the world.

I said I was a New Zealand author working on a historical crime story and looking for a Phyllis, whose parents were Eric and Edith Thompson. 'Eric had quite a dramatic family background,' I wrote, 'with his father dying of apparent strychnine poisoning in 1892. I have no idea, of course, how much of this Phyllis may know as Eric seems to have been somewhat estranged from the English side of his family.' Was Phyllis his wife, I asked?

His reply was quick and friendly. 'Yes,' he said – and he would pass on to her any more information I cared to send. But he added a caution: 'She has mixed feelings about all this but I have given her your contact information. While I am likely more interested in your research than she, I will leave the ball in her court to respond.'

The big question was how to word my request. Carefully, I related some of what I knew about the 'Waikomiti mystery' and asked if she would be kind enough to share with me any information she might have.

'I would be most interested,' I wrote, 'to learn what Eric knew of his beginnings and how that knowledge might have affected his life. I think he may have had a hard time on the fringes of the Thompsons' world and missed out on the emotional support his older brother clearly received.' I included photos of Eric and her Uncle Alfgar and her grandmother, Alice. I took a deep breath and pressed *Send*.

Then I waited. And waited ...

A week went by. I grew anxious. If my news was going to intrigue her, surely she would have replied by now. Finally, twelve days later, in it came – just a few brief lines. They made me slump at the keyboard and sigh.

I had surprised her, she wrote. 'It has taken me some time to absorb the information.' And then: 'While I find the history interesting, I feel no connection to past events. My father died when I was young and I have no photos or additional information that would help you. In your writing you may mention that Eric had a daughter, but I would prefer privacy and to not be identified.'

There was so little to glean from that response. Her reference to 'past events' might hint at some prior awareness, or perhaps she was just referring to the contents of my earlier email. It could have been a topic scarcely mentioned in her youth, possibly laden with a sense of being a secret best not talked about, and therefore best forgotten. Many families handle painful episodes that way – thinking it better to leave them in the past rather than rip off the band-aid to expose old wounds. I had no way of knowing.

Sadly, I messaged Carolyn to tell her I was at the end of the line. She came back with: 'Wow, that's a lead balloon, but I guess she has her reasons.'

Just few weeks later I was in the midst of a painful episode of my own. My husband, Pete, died. He'd been going downhill all the time I had been working on the book, which was two years at that point. It had been hard to get him out of the house for even a short walk. He had an incurable condition, interstitial lung disease, and his energy had plummeted as his breathing grew more and more difficult.

When he picked up an infection, I was told I must take him to hospital. At once. He grew worse. Finally, in ICU, they pushed oxygen into him through a tight-fitting face mask, but in the end the only way to ease his terrible struggle for air was to administer morphine. Told there were now no other options for giving him comfort, he was only just able to agree. 'My lungs are stuffed,' he gasped. 'I just want to fade away.' And he did. A few days later I stood at his bedside at dawn with my daughters. It was Valentine's Day.

It's a terrible thing to gaze at a loved one's chest, expecting it to rise, *willing* it to lift, and seeing no movement at all. I held on to his bare left arm. His hand was already icy, his elbow chilling fast.

I remembered then the sentence spoken by a neighbour at William Thompson's bedside. 'He is dead and cold – cold as clay.' It was strange that I should recall that sentence at such an awful moment, but I did. How bizarre it was to link such an old death scene with this most acutely sorrowful one. I did then know, however, exactly how that coldness feels.

GRIEF IS A GRUELLING LIFE STAGE. We'd been married for many years and I missed Pete hugely. Now the house was eerily, totally empty of any other heartbeat but mine. It was hard to get used to.

For close to a year I couldn't write anything. I busied myself by working extra hard in a community role. I could function well enough when the work was just about business, but when it came to my own writing, there was just no water in the well. I felt hollowed out, dry as a bone. I was embarrassed that I still had Nick Frost's box of Thompson memorabilia. Months had ticked by and it was still sitting in my office. It took me ages to even email Nick to say: 'Sorry you've not heard from me, and here's why.'

'Please be in no hurry,' he replied. 'It will just go back in the attic!' Covid lockdowns were still affecting courier deliveries all over the world. Eventually I sent it off with my heart in my mouth, terrified it might go missing in the chaos, and six weeks later it finally arrived at Nick's door.

Phyllis's rejection had made me think there wasn't much point in carrying on with the story, and I was struggling to think of a satisfying ending. But slowly my urge to finish it returned. The book was only half done and I hate leaving projects incomplete. I wanted to push past William Thompson's death and get on with the what-happened-afterwards chunk.

Eventually I returned to the keyboard, still trying to bring the story full circle. Then, just as I was nearing the end of what I knew, Carolyn idly googled Phyllis again, just in case any fresh news had popped up – and was startled to be confronted by newspaper obituaries. Phyllis, the last of the Thompson line, had died only a few weeks earlier, on 22 January 2022, in Sonoma, Northern California.

'No!' I said when Carolyn called me with the news. 'That's awful.' I was deeply affected by the passing of this woman I had never met. I was so sad for her husband and friends. All hope of ever talking with her was gone. It was slightly spooky, too, on a personal level. Phyllis and I were both born in June of 1945, on opposite sides of the Pacific. Her death was a reminder of my own mortality.

There were long, affectionate tributes to her in Sonoma newspapers. How well loved she was. Said one friend: 'She left an impact on our community and our hearts in some of the most charming, disarming and lovable ways. That said, she self-professed that she "did not play well with others", when it came to boards, committees and the spotlight.'

So, that aversion to exposure explained some of her reluctance to engage with me. I emailed my sympathy to John and he came back quickly. Even better, he was open to a phone call and we talked a few weeks later.

He had kept my earlier emails to her because he'd thought she might change her mind about learning more of her dad's history. But she had never wanted to talk about it. In sorting her effects, he had found nothing new. He did find her baby book, made by Phyllis's mother, with a family tree full of names from her mother's Italian side of the family. Eric's side was completely blank. 'That was interesting,' said John. 'I thought maybe Edith had no information.'

There it was. More than half a century after the dreadful death on Parker Road, Eric had been unwilling or unable to share his history with his wife. Even in something so innocent and private as a baby book, there was a gaping void. No ancestry, no names, no background. Silence.

Oh, mysterious Eric, presumably never speaking of his difficult past. He had no reason to be silent or embarrassed by it, but maybe a lifetime of striving to be his own man, untainted by the old murder story, meant he couldn't bring himself to share his secrets even with Edith. Which meant his daughter grew up oblivious to the details of her dad's life. Or perhaps she knew just enough to be convinced it was a story she did not want to explore.

Every so often I pondered on approaching her a second time. I thought she might have liked to learn how Eric had gone from Winnipeg to Detroit alone when he was just sixteen. How he'd forged his own path. How far he'd travelled. I thought she might have been proud he'd done so well. But due to her reluctance, I'd hesitated.

Now it was too late.

'Because Phyllis is gone now, do you think it's acceptable for me to name her in my book?' I asked John. Yes, he said. Given that she could no longer be disturbed by it, he could see no reason for continued secrecy.

Phyllis Thompson lost her father, Eric, when she was just six but enjoyed happy teenage years in San Francisco.

His surname is Gurney, and so now I could say it was hers too. They had no children. So finally, the story I'd heard at the beginning of my search, that the Thompson family had no survivors, had come true. She was the last one.

Phyllis worked in science education but never lost her love of dance, She taught lively fitness classes well into her seventies.

After Eric's death, his widow sold the family's suburban home and took Phyllis to the city, moving in with her mother and an unmarried aunt. Edith had to return to work and needed daily care for her daughter. Phyllis grew up close to two girl cousins – Lynn and Nanette. She majored in biology and dance at San Francisco State University and then had a long high-school science teaching career.

Dance was an enduring passion. She taught Jazzercise for twenty years and then became a 'spin' teacher. At seventy-plus she was running high-energy gym bike sessions full of vim and laughter. They were so popular, says John, that people 'fought to get in'. She was famous for announcing in her classes whatever American national day it was. There's always something to celebrate there. An annual online calendar (nationaltoday.com), lists them all. Fun ones in January, for instance, include Bloody Mary Day, Apple Gifting Day, Polar Bear Plunge Day, Hot Sauce Day, Polka Dot Day and Beer Can Appreciation Day.

John and Phyllis Gurney at their 1978 wedding.

She would get off her saddle sometimes and dance around the room. 'Phyllis,' said a friend, 'was the spoonful of sugar that made the medicine, as in exercise, go down.'

There was more: she'd not wanted children of her own but supported causes ranging from animal welfare to the arts and education. Phyllis loved going to the theatre and dancing with John. She had also been bungee jumping, mountain climbing and spelunking. She hated high-tech (her only mobile was an ancient flip phone) and detested TV – relishing instead quiet nights in front of the fire with a good book and a vodka cocktail. The Gurneys were wed for more than forty years, but John could tell me only one memory she had shared with him about Eric. 'She remembered sitting on his lap while he read to her the words in newspaper cartoons. All her life she read daily papers and still liked cartoons and doing Sudoku.'

At seventy-six – an age when few women are still gym-goers – she kept on teaching fitness classes despite noticing some pain and numbness. At first a neurologist put it down to a pinched nerve. It didn't go away. Finally, she taught what would turn out to be her last class and then kept an appointment for an MRI. The shocking result – she had a glioblastoma, an aggressive brain tumour.

The Gurneys at a 2019 party.
Photos: John Gurney collection

Surgery followed swiftly but only some of the cancer could be removed. She was left in pain and without the use of her left arm and leg. She was told there was no cure and that intense radiotherapy and chemotherapy might give her only another eighteen to twenty-four months.

Phyllis took charge. If the full life she loved couldn't continue, she preferred not to be here at all. Instead, she chose to make use of California's End of Life Option, a law that allows terminally ill people to self-administer medication to end their own lives, with the consent of two physicians. Locals call it the death-with-dignity act.

John was not surprised. 'We'd discussed it once, so I could have predicted it. She never wavered. She was strong and committed.' And she did not want to wait – the time from diagnosis of her tumour to her passing was just sixteen days.

One of her newspaper tributes said: 'She laughed at herself easily and kept life easy. But if something serious came up, then her calmer head prevailed – she made a plan and executed the plan.'

I told John I was very sad not to have met her, but also how delighted I was that after all the troubles of her ancestors, she had had a beautiful life. Her father's forlorn childhood and her grandmother's New Zealand scandal had happened in a distant century. That old story of love gone wrong was nothing to do with her; Eric's girl had grown up in fresh, bright American fields.

She couldn't have planned her passing more perfectly for, coincidentally, the day of her death was America's Celebration of Life Day.

There was no traditional funeral. John gave the undertaker her wedding ring and a few other tokens she wanted put in her coffin for cremation. 'She wore almost no other jewellery,' John told me. 'Phyllis wasn't a shopper. She liked things simple.'

Later, he and some friends took a boat out on San Francisco Bay one calm day and scattered her ashes on a sapphire sea.

A few days after our conversation, I received a surprise invitation. Phyllis was smiling out at me from the screen. It read: 'Phyllis would NOT like to invite you to a celebration of her life because she wouldn't want all the fuss. But I, John Gurney, am inviting you to come make a fuss with me.' He and friends were planning a special event in her honour. They selected 11 June. That would be six months after her death, an oh-so-suitable date because it would be Making Life Beautiful Day.

'You are welcome to join us,' the message went on, 'which will annoy Phyllis greatly.' An additional cheeky footnote said, 'BYOK – Bring Your Own Kleenex.'

I had flights booked within days.

CHAPTER THIRTY-SIX

It was a golden midsummer afternoon on 11 June 2022 when hundreds gathered to farewell Phyllis Gurney at a community centre in Sonoma – a lovely expanse of grape-growing country about an hour north of San Francisco.

John hosted the event, often choking up as he spoke, but there was laughter along with the tears. He talked of Phyllis's joy, enthusiasm and great strength. Of how dearly she'd loved all her friends. He wore a shirt specially embroidered for the day, with 'H to H' spelt out across the back. Referencing her dislike for screen-only contact, it stood for human-to-human.

He noted that in tidying her things afterwards, he found a box on her desk. Inside it she had kept words to live by. 'There were sentiments she would practise in her life on a daily basis – words like gratitude, sharing, encouragement, good deeds, listening, giving, forgiveness,' he said. 'If you can practise them yourself, you'll be a wonderful person. Just like Phyllis.'

He wanted the crowd to know the importance of having hard conversations with loved ones when it comes to death and dying. 'It was not easy helping Phyllis fulfil her wishes but I understood her and we talked about it, so we were able to move through this – what she wanted – and that was important. I just encourage you to talk to your loved ones, understand that when stuff happens, you want to be prepared.'

Before I'd flown to California, I'd offered to speak at the gathering, and John duly called me up to the stage. 'This person wins a very special prize because she's travelled the farthest – from New Zealand!' It was a warm and welcoming crowd; they clapped and cheered. 'She never got to meet Phyllis,' said John. 'But she's going to share a story with you, so sit right back and you'll hear a tale.'

'You'll be thinking,' I began, 'who is this woman with the odd accent? Mine is a face you've never seen. I'm a stranger to all of you. And I was a stranger to Phyllis as well. But a while ago I shocked her to the core by telling her I knew quite a lot about her father, because I was writing about him.'

So I told them of her dad Eric's secret and difficult ancestry. I knew their own ancestors would have been lured by the American dream. 'Phyllis's grandparents went in search of the New Zealand dream,' I said. 'It ended tragically, but one hundred and thirty years later I can see today what a full and happy life was lived here by their last remaining grandchild. How proud of her they would have been.'

Afterwards, people told me how wonderful Phyllis was. 'I adored her,' said one woman. 'We all did,' added someone else. They could not believe how someone apparently so healthy could have gone so swiftly from their lives.

We toasted her with beautiful pale Carneros Rosé wine – Phyllis's favourite – made by friends who run the local Three Fat Guys winery. John gifted me a bottle to take home. The Gurneys tended pinot noir grapes on twelve hundred vines next to their ranch-style home, and the wine was made from the last harvest she had a hand in processing. They made olive oil, too and John says that Phyllis put 'sweat and effort' into both products. Her grandparents struggled to grow apples in Auckland, but she was a gardening queen.

I MET two other people that day who'd been close to Phyllis – her cousin, Lynn Ward, and her personal physician, Brian Sebastian. They had more to tell me, but the room was so noisy that we agreed to chat later by Zoom. And so, some weeks later, we did.

Phyllis had almost no memory of Eric, but Lynn was two years older and still remembers him well. At last, I could talk to someone who had known him!

'He was quite handsome,' Lynn said. 'He had a full head of salt-and-pepper grey hair, a slight physique, wore wire-rimmed glasses – was distinguished looking. He had a memorable, resonant voice and a playful, dry wit.' She recalls him looking relaxed in shirt sleeves, usually with a cigarette holder. He liked to smoke. Back then, nobody knew the dangers of sucking in lungfuls of nicotine. He had no idea what his habit was doing to his heart.

'It's many, many years ago, but I know my parents and Eric would socialise, go out in San Francisco to dinner and go dancing. They had wonderful times. I know they did because they would get the giggles over something. Eric was funny.' He looked buttoned down, she said, 'but he wasn't.'

Eric on holiday in 1948, little Phyllis alongside, living his American dream far from the old New Zealand poisoning story about which he never spoke. Photo: Lynn Ward collection

His death in 1951 rocked the family. 'I remember a very emotional time. There weren't many of us – we lived near each other and we were close.'

She recalls Eric's wife, Edith, as 'fun and gutsy', a tennis player who also loved horseback riding. 'We really enjoyed her. Everybody did. She was a strong lady – though devastated when Eric died. Now I can look back and see she was mourning and grieving, but even as a kid I just knew this was not good. But she got her act together and was successful in her own right. I know she travelled with friends; they would go to dude ranches and on ski trips.'

However, in 1979, Edith's heart would also fail her. 'It was sad because she was so looking forward to retiring at sixty-five. She did, and she had this list of I'm-gonna items, but six months later she had a massive heart attack and was gone.'

Eric's widow Edith in the early '60s with her daughter Phyllis, then aged about 12. Photo: Lynn Ward collection

Lynn believes Phyllis's push for lifelong fitness was influenced by her parents' heart troubles. 'She watched her diet and exercise levels. She was upset in the last five years that, darn it, she had to take cholesterol medication! It made her mad. She was doing everything she should because "with my history, that's what's going to get me".' But, of course, her fitness could not save her from brain cancer.

Lynn was shocked when her cousin fell ill. 'I exercised as much as she did – we always compared notes. When we talked one day late in 2021, she was having trouble with her left foot and lower leg and was seeing a neurologist. For a while it improved, and then she said it was right back where it had been.'

Early 2022 delivered her grim diagnosis and then the surgery, with its negative outcome. Lynn lives in San Jose, one hundred and forty kilometres from Phyllis's home, but she was in constant touch with John after the operation. One day Phyllis called her. 'You could have knocked me onto the floor. It was almost like she had a script in front of her and she said, "Lynn, I wanted to talk to you to tell you that I have chosen to die with dignity." That's precisely what she said – *I have chosen*. I was dumbfounded and said, "Oh, Phyllis." I thought for a moment and then told her, "I understand that is your decision, and I respect that." I could have commented and said, *well I wouldn't*. But I didn't.' It was a typical Phyllis choice, says Lynn. 'She made up her mind and it was the situation according to her.'

Lynn had cared for her late husband through a long illness they both knew was terminal, and her eyes glistened with emotion as she said she believed choosing to die was the last thing she herself would do – 'I have my faith. I'm a good Catholic, and so I don't think that's my choice – though, who knows ...'

Phyllis's choice was tough on her friends too. Brian Sebastian hadn't just been her physician. He and his partner, Richard Mabe, were long-time friends of both the Gurneys. There was no way he could have written the prescription for the deadly euthanasia drugs.

'I had never been asked to do that before,' Brian told me. 'I had mixed feelings about writing it for anybody. The act of actually doing it, assisting someone to end their life, was an emotional conflict for me – and it would be especially hard doing it for a friend.'

Instead, Phyllis turned to hospital oncologists. 'She got them on board with her decision very quickly,' said Brian. 'They went through the process. Two physicians need to interview you and then there's a waiting period to allow time for the patient to possibly reconsider. There was a two-week waiting period, which annoyed her. She said, "I want to do it right now." Then abruptly the law changed, and it became just a forty-eight-hour waiting period.' She wanted to wait no longer.

It happened on a Saturday at a care facility – 'a really nice, calm place'. Phyllis asked Brian to visit her before the day she intended to die. 'She was not going to let people see her at all, but she asked me to go and I thought, God, what does she want to ask me? Is she going to ask me what's it like, and what am I going to say? By this time the ball was rolling, the medications had been ordered, she was situated in place. I went and sat with her and she was basically telling me, "Brian, I don't want to live this way. This is not me. I don't want people remembering me like this."

'She was justifying her choice, but she didn't have to convince me at that point. I knew. I understood, of course. I sat with her for a while, and then she asked me to be there when she took her own life. I told her, "I'll be here with you, of course, but I'm bringing Richard with me because I need him here, you know?" She said okay.'

Brian and Richard had both wondered about her resistance to knowing her father's background. 'Richard suspected her dad was in the mafia or something, or there was some other secret. We didn't know how much she knew or if she knew nothing.' It still puzzles him. 'How can you not feel connected to the past somehow? It is shaping you in some way. But no, she didn't want to talk about it.'

Lynn also told me that Phyllis always lived for the moment, even as a girl. 'She didn't ever look over her shoulder.' But none of that mattered now.

There were only a few people at her bedside – her husband, John, of course, plus Brian and Richard and another close friend.

'No physician or nurse is supposed to be present,' explained Brian. 'I was there in an unofficial capacity. I wasn't administering anything.' Under Californian law, people wishing to die have to take the medication themselves. 'You can't have it administered. No one can pour it down your throat.' In New Zealand, patients can elect to be given the fatal drug dose intravenously or to swallow it themselves. In California, there is no choice.

Brian described how surreal and difficult it was. There was even a darkly comical moment. 'Richard and I had offered to bring coffee for everybody.' It had been their habit to bring café-made drinks to all their get-togethers. 'I mean, what does one bring to a friend's suicide?' He waved his hands as he mocked the dreadful awkwardness of it all. 'We'll bring the coffee!'

Once they entered the room, of course, the scene was profoundly serious. John was tearful. As a first step, he had already given Phyllis an anti-nausea drug. In California, the patient must swallow a vile-tasting toxic mixture – a range of powders mixed into juice. Phyllis had been pre-warned about its unpleasantness. Anti-nausea medication serves to stop people throwing it back up.

As Brian remembers it, Phyllis was unflappable and calm. As awful as it was for everyone else, she wanted no ceremony or emotion.

'I think what impressed me so much was her absolute determination. Phyllis, just very matter of factly, said, "Is it time yet?" Yes, we said, it's time. John goes to mix the stuff. It's a bunch of powders and you have to mix it in juice. He's mixing it, and he's breaking down as he's doing it. He's just shaking. We were all surrounding the bed, and he brings it over to her and she takes it and slurps it down. At the first swallow she said, "Echh! that's awful!" John said, "They told us it would taste very bad, Phyllis. You've got to drink it quickly." She was slurping to a point where she was making sure she was going to get every molecule down. She was not going to take any risks that this might not work.'

She looked at Brian and said, 'So what happens now?' He suggested she should just lie back and go to sleep. 'Okay, good,' she said. 'She put her head back and that was it. She didn't move, she was completely serene.' And very soon, she was gone.

How strange it is that the manner of her death echoed something of the way young William Thompson had died in Auckland so long ago. It was, of course, a different kind of poisoning in utterly different circumstances. When William expired in 1892, he suffered a lonely, horrible death in a dark country house, killed by strychnine a jury decided was delivered by a man he'd wrongly believed to be a loyal friend.

Phyllis, who was (officially at least) William's granddaughter, lived a good long life until her incurable illness struck. Then she made her own decision. She died intentionally and peacefully, one hundred and thirty years later. Using legal lethal drugs, she ended her own life on a bright morning of her choosing, surrounded by people who dearly loved her. In a way, the story had come full circle. It was, I thought, a kind of triumph for the woman who liked to live life her way.

Eric and Edith picnicking in Canada in 1947 four years
after they were wed. Photo: Lynn Ward collection

CHAPTER THIRTY-SEVEN

There was one more thing I wanted to do before flying home. Having begun this story with a visit to William Thompson's Auckland grave, I was keen to see Eric's headstone in California. A local friend, Uta Jehnich, took me to Golden Gate National Cemetery, a vast resting place in San Bruno for 145,000 veterans who served in various American wars, and some of their family members. It was daunting – how to find one grave amongst so many?

By the entry gate we found an ATM-like machine. When I poked in Eric's name, it came up with a number and spat out a fuzzy map. He was in Section L, but even that one area was huge and the grave numbers followed no apparent plan. Uta and I went wandering amongst the rows of white headstones. It was very windy. San Francisco's airport is nearby. Jets roared overhead as we zig-zagged back and forth and the ground shimmered with American flags flapping round our knees. It was soon after Memorial Day, when teams of volunteer scouts place lines of small flags on sticks next to headstones in every military cemetery across the United States.

It reminded me, for a moment, of how untended grass had thrashed around my ankles back in Waikumete Cemetery when I'd stood at the grave of Alexander Scott, whose nineteenth-century crime had triggered this long journey of mine. Different graveyard. Different century.

Author Lindsey Dawson searching for Eric's grave in the vast Golden Gate National Cemetery. Photo: Uta Jehnich

Then suddenly, there he was! Eric V Thompson, a veteran of World War I. His name is on the front of the stone; Edith's is on the back.

I'd wanted to take flowers but the only florist near my hotel was closed due to illness. Covid was rife in San Francisco at the time. But I did have a much more meaningful token – a few dried sprigs of tōtara from the property in Ōrātia, where Eric was conceived. Carolyn gave them to me to take to California. The leaves were from no ordinary tōtara tree but a Hall's tōtara, a species named after a member of Eric's own family. Remember Mr Hall, the Thames chemist (and keen botanist) whose home Alice stayed in when she was pregnant with Eric? Hall was a great-uncle of Eric's, and so I was able to deliver a few tiny leaves connected to his forebears.

Eric Thompson's grave, with a sprig of Hall's Totara from a tree that stands on the Auckland land formerly called Sunnydale, where his father Willam had once longed to thrive. Photo: Author

We put them on the headstone to take a photo, but the wild weather made it tricky. Uta held them down while I manned my iPhone, but the second she let go, *whoosh!* Off they flew, except for one game little leaf that somehow stuck as if by magic, clinging on just long enough for my button click.

Uta had thoughtfully brought along dried sage, intending that we should light it to waft fragrant smoke over the grave as a blessing, but the wind was so strong we couldn't light a match – though back in the shelter of her car we did fill the interior with its lovely pungency.

'Did you bring a reading?' she said. 'Poetry, maybe?' I hadn't. Just as well she knew how to do things properly. In a trice she found an online New Zealand poetry site on which authors read their own work out loud. 'So, who would you like?' she asked. I suggested Kevin Ireland, and soon his recorded voice rang out tinnily on her phone from across the world as he read his small poem 'Thorn and Wind'. On that blustery day, it seemed appropriate. Eric probably never heard a New Zealand voice in all his adult life, but it felt right for marking the life of a man whose turbulent life had been so affected by the coming and going of love. Here's how it goes:

> on the spring day
> that love was born
> the wind whipped
> the budding thorn
> on the winter's day
> that love was dead
> the thorn ripped
> and the wind bled

Lynn Ward can remember Eric's burial in 1951. It was a formal military ceremony that included the slow ritual folding of the American flag into a neat red, white and blue triangle for the family to keep as a memento. Though she was only eight, she recalls someone tried to hand it to her. She pointed to her cousin Phyllis, for as Eric's daughter the flag was hers to hold. Twenty-eight years later, Lynn and Phyllis were back there again, attending the funeral of Edith, Eric's widow.

Every family's story is complicated – and in Eric's case, more than most. He withheld many secrets from the people he loved. But his silence may have been an act of love – for what girl would want to grow up thinking she may be a murderer's granddaughter? And while Phyllis may have known little or nothing of her dad's difficult childhood, none of us can ever know what *really* went on in our ancestors' lives. If we can grab some contentment here and now, perhaps that's all that matters.

In the end, all you can do with old headstones is lay your hand upon them, bless the souls commemorated there and walk away into your own future.

EPILOGUE: OTHER CHARACTERS' LIVES

THIS BOOK'S FIRST PART, ABOUT THE DEATH OF WILLIAM Thompson and the execution of Alexander Scott, introduced many people who disappeared from the story after that. Once Thompson and Scott were dead and widow Alice and her sons had left New Zealand, everyone else carried on with their lives.

So, what did they move on to? Dr Roberton, who had been called out to William's death scene and done the post-mortem, must have left the trial behind him with relief, for he was about to get married. The bride was a Miss Wilkie. A grand wedding it was too. The *Observer* breathlessly described the bride's 'beautiful robe of deep ivory colour'. The bodice, sleeves and Watteau train were of velvet, and the silk and satin skirt had a ruched hem dotted with posies of orange blossoms.

The couple would rear a remarkable family of three sons and a daughter, all of whom became doctors. Two of the sons joined British regiments to fight in World War I, and their daughter,

Isabel, gained her medical degree at Edinburgh University in 1922.

As I read about their lives, I began to realise I was familiar with Roberton's name. He was one of the founders, in 1904, of Diocesan School for Girls, so he'd had a hand in my teenage years. His Isabel was obviously brilliant – she followed in his footsteps at university and was the first doctor produced by 'Dio'. I was not a stellar pupil. I recall thinking at age sixteen, 'Thank God that's over', as I walked out its gates for the last time. Dr Roberton would not have been impressed.

As for the others, Justice Conolly stayed on the Bench. A man of strict moral views, he favoured long sentences for abortionists. Years after Scott's trial, he presided over a case in which a doctor was found not guilty of procuring an abortion. Conolly was appalled when women in the gallery cheered the jury's decision.

He was 'disgusted to see women leading the applause', noted author Alison Clarke in her book *Born to a Changing World: Childbirth in Nineteenth-Century New Zealand*. Conolly had said in his summing up that 'the birth-rate of this colony was not what it should be'. Back then, of course, godly people were intent on obeying the Book of Genesis injunction to 'go forth and multiply' (Genesis 1:28).

He certainly did his best. His wife, Emily, bore him fourteen children, of whom only nine made it to adulthood. That probably helps explain his dismissive comments about Alice, owner of the scandalous 'preventative pessary'.

On the other hand, as a politician he had supported legislation to protect property rights of married women. 'Why should a woman when she marries lose her identity?' he asked. 'Why should she become the mere housekeeper, the servant, the nurse of man?'

By 1900 his wife had died and an unmarried daughter, Daisy, took on his care, no doubt (ironically) becoming his housekeeper, servant and nurse. His biography in *Te Ara: The Encyclopedia of New Zealand* says he grew 'deaf, slightly incoherent of speech and noticeably crabby' as he grew older. This must have irked his peers, for as he neared his eightieth birthday, a petition was organised to bring in mandatory retirement for judges at age eighty. Conolly resigned from the Bench in 1903, at eighty-one, and died five years later.

Most of the lawyers involved in the case had good futures ahead. They weren't just smart barristers. Joseph Tole, said one newspaper report, 'plays the fiddle like an angel' and was a very good tenor too.

Remember Frederick Baume, who was in charge of representing the family the day after William's death? He was enraged with the police when Scott was arrested. In 1907, fourteen years after Scott's trial, he would take the oath as a King's Counsel on the same day as Tole, in the first group of New Zealand lawyers to earn that honour.

Theo Cooper rose to the greatest heights. He was on his way to becoming a Supreme Court judge and would earn a knighthood. When he died in Hamilton in 1925, Archdeacon Cowie (the same Cowie who had once tried to counsel Alexander Scott as he awaited his hanging) said Cooper 'had not enjoyed the evening of his days in the way one would have liked, for he had worn himself out with work'.

A long life was not granted to Edwin Hesketh, however. The Scott trial was the last time in which he would act as lead counsel in a major trial. Aged fifty then, his hearing was already failing. He'd hoped for an acquittal. Instead, he and his brother Samuel could only watch as Scott's coffin went into the ground.

When Edwin died five years later, Justice Conolly had kind words for him, noting everyone's regret for how his deafness had afflicted him. Edwin's funeral was huge, with papers noting the music played, the number of wreaths (fifty), the hymns sung and even a description of the casket – 'oak mounted with silver'.

Samuel Hesketh worked on, becoming senior partner of Hesketh, Richmond, Adams and Cocker. The *Auckland Star* noted his sixtieth wedding anniversary in 1938, by which time he'd also put in sixty years with the firm.

The case was a boost for police careers too. Detectives Chrystal and Grace both featured in a letter of commendation by Inspector Broham to his bosses. 'The proofs of guilt they procured formed by far the most important part of the evidence for the prosecution,' he wrote.

Writing this story brought closure for me, too. Telling another family's tale prompted me to revisit my own mother's grave for the first time in fifty years. After all my decades of absence, it was about time. I thought about her with love and gratitude, and left for her a tiny posy of fragrant lavender and rosemary.

I was also slow to say a final goodbye to my husband, Pete. It took me ages to be able to face it, but finally, three years after his memorial service, I gathered my daughters and grandchildren for a summer visit to his favourite beach where, at last, we scattered his ashes, hugged each other, told stories and filled our hearts with the balm of recalling so many good times shared.

SOURCES AND GRATITUDE

My primary sources of information about the death of William Thompson and the trial of Alexander Scott were digitised newspapers in the wonderful repository of New Zealand history – Papers Past. I also looked at the Australian equivalent, Trove, and newspapers.com in the United States.

As I went deeper to find out more about the Thompson family, I was blessed to be granted access to family records kept by Nick Frost, of Monmouth, Wales, two-times great nephew of William Thompson.

Twenty years ago he had also shared them with his cousin, the late Monica Leat, who was then studying their family history. William had also been *her* great-great uncle. She sent her research to Carolyn Melling, who was living in William Thompson's old home, and Carolyn kindly made it all available to me along with accounts she, too, had written about the 'Waikomiti mystery'. Carolyn also made great cups of tea, excellent cake, shared her passion for flowers and gardening and was endlessly generous in information sharing.

I owe Nick Frost so much for trusting me with his treasured family pictures and documents and waiting patiently for me to return it all many months later. My thanks, too, to David Leat, who assisted with recall of his late wife Monica's work on the Thompson story.

Appreciation also goes to John Gurney, Lynn Ward, Brian Meredith, Richard Mabe, Marcia Nelson and the many kind friends of Phyllis Gurney in Sonoma who made me feel welcome at her celebration of life.

Researching the Thompson family took me into many online sources. Genealogy sites can only deliver so much, however, so I'm indebted to many people who love history and could deliver more context and detail – such as Auckland researcher Lynley Stone; genealogist Freda Walker, of Rothbury, England; enthusiasts at the British Isles Family History Society of Greater Ottawa, Canada; and volunteers at the Mansfield Historical Society in Victoria, Australia.

I also received help from the Walsall Leather Museum in Staffordshire; Father Hudson's Care in Birmingham; Auckland's Catholic Enquiry Centre; the New Zealand Maritime Museum; State Library Victoria in Melbourne; the Alexander Turnbull Library in Wellington; and the New Zealand Medical Association's publications editor, who supplied biographical details for doctors involved in the murder trial.

My regular meetings with Auckland writing friends kept me going whenever my energy flagged. Thanks, Cath Mayo, Weng-Wai Chan, Lisa Grace and Robin Harding for your kindness, advice and perceptive critiques. The late Stephen Stratford assessed the manuscript and offered good advice. Wellington editor Paul Stewart gave my manuscript the discipline and decent grammar it needed. I appreciated publishing assistance from Martin Taylor of Digital Strategies and proofreading by Rosemary Hepozden of The Word Factory.

Wellington law student Hanna Malloch researched some of the oddities of nineteenth-century New Zealand law for me. If any errors exist, they will be down to me. Document examiner and graphologist Mike Maran took me through the mysteries of handwriting analysis.

Before his passing in 2023, poet Kevin Ireland invited me to a cheerful pub lunch with literary friends and kindly gave me permission to use his poem, 'Thorn and Wind', from *Anzac Day: Selected Poems* (Hazard Press, 1997).

And, as always, my lovely daughters Dee and Joey did me the great service of keeping on asking, 'How's the book going?'

FURTHER READING

Useful books included *The Mysterious Death of Jane Stanford*, Robert WP Cutler MD, Stanford University Press Books, 2003; *Rock College: An unofficial history of Mount Eden Prison*, by Mark Derby, Massey University Press, 2020; *The Poisoner's Handbook: Murder and the Birth of Forensic Medicine in Jazz Age New York*, by Deborah Blum, Penguin, 2011; *Born to a Changing World: Childbirth in Nineteenth-Century New Zealand*, by Alison Clarke, Bridget Williams Books, 2012; *Behind the Dispensing Screen: Early New Zealand Pharmacists*, written and published by Murray R Frost, Hamilton, 2003; *Urban Village: The Story of Ponsonby, Freemans Bay and St Mary's Bay*, by Jenny Carlyon and Diana Morrow, Random House, 2008; *Once ... the Wilderness* by John T Diamond, VH Wilkinson, 1953; and *The Lonely Grave: What happened to the man and the boy buried in this grave in the Ōrātia Cemetery* by Carolyn Melling, ref.993.23 MELL, Waitākere Central Library Research Centre, 2005.

ABOUT THE AUTHOR

Lindsey Dawson is a former journalist and magazine editor who has also worked in TV and radio. She has authored nine previous books. This one was inspired by a murder trial she stumbled over when researching her most recent novel, *Scarlet & Magenta*, about Victorian settlers' lives in New Zealand. That story was fiction. This one actually happened.

www.lindseydawson.com

ALSO BY LINDSEY DAWSON

"THE PERFECT BLEND OF ROMANCE, HISTORY AND DRAMA."

Oh, how could it be *such a sin* for a woman to have a mind of her own?

In the 1880s, misbehaving wives were asking for trouble. Building a raw new town was hard enough without free-thinking females upsetting local society. Violet arrives in the Bay of Plenty with a scandalous past and an aching heart. She befriends a kindred spirit, Anna, and also catches the eye of footloose Rupert – a friend and business rival of Anna's husband.

In Victorian pioneer towns, it doesn't do to speak your mind or seek unseemly delights. Angry words are soon flying in banks and bedrooms, with reputations and marriages at risk. There are secrets to keep and lost loved ones to find.

"Let me pose this simple question: 'What endures longest – blood ties or friendship?'

"My temper is so unpredictable. I keep it buckled down so hard,

but then moments erupt that are so provoking it's as if someone has lit a wick in me."

"I was appalled when I heard what had happened. It could have been the end of you. And then I don't know what I would have done."

Scarlet & Magenta vividly reveals the trials and pleasures of colonial life and explores the question of what matters most in all of our lives – blood ties or friendship. Set mostly in late 19th century New Zealand, the story also includes telling moments in London, Bombay and Sydney that reveal Britain's eager appetite for sending its citizens out to rule the empire even as far as New Zealand – Victoria's most far-flung colony. And how settlers had to put aside their cultural conditioning from "home" as they struggled to build new lives in places so different from everything they'd left behind.

Shortlisted for the New Zealand Heritage Book Awards, it has been dubbed (by review site nzbooklovers.co.nz) "the perfect blend of romance, history and drama." Lindsey Dawson has use used real-life letters by an ancestor to create this magnificent story.

"Lindsey Dawson has a gift for transporting the reader back in time. Witty and absorbing, filled with strong women and their secrets, this is a real treat for lovers of New Zealand historical fiction."
– **Author Nicky Pellegrino**

"Dawson's chatty style makes Scarlet & Magenta *an entertaining read. The novel's insight into what it was like to be a woman in that time and place will leave most of us grateful we're not, even if Dawson makes it clear that some attitudes haven't moved on much."*
– **Catherine Robertson,** *NZ Listener*

OTHER BOOKS BY THE AUTHOR

Fiction

Angel Baby

Lipstick in the Dust

Scarlet & Magenta

Non-fiction

Pearls: Let Out the Wise Soul Within You

Wise Up: How to be Fearless and Fulfilled in Midlife

The Elemental You: Discover and Delight in Your Primal Personality

Crack Your Life: How to Write Memoir That Rocks

The Answer: How Nature Can Help You when Life Seems Too Hard

The Next Book of Home Decorating